All the Way Home

All the Way Home

MAX BRAITHWAITE

McClelland and Stewart

The Canadian Publishers
McClelland and Stewart Limited
25 Hollinger Road, Toronto M4B 3G2

Canadian Cataloguing in Publication Data

Braithwaite, Max, 1911–
All the way home

ISBN 0-7710-1612-3

I. Title.

PS8503.R34A73 1986 C813′.54 C86-093281-8
PR9199.3.B735A73 1986

This is a work of fiction. Any resemblance to persons living or dead is purely coincidental.

Printed in Canada

To Aileen

Chapter One

"You can buckle up your seat belt," the pretty stewardess said. "We'll be starting our descent soon." When the passenger didn't turn away from the window, she persisted, laying a hand lightly on his shoulder. "Sir, there's no hurry, but don't forget to buckle up."

"What? Oh yes, thank you." Hugh Windmar looked up at her and saw beautiful brown hair, wide-set brown eyes, and a friendly smile. She must be about nineteen, the same age as Elaine had been. Elaine had been a toucher, too.

Hugh was a lean man in a neat, expensive suit. He looked as though he jogged every day, although he'd never run more than a couple of blocks in his life. He had a thin, straight nose, alert eyes, and a good thatch of hair, dyed brown. He was sixty-five years old and looked fifty. He was riding first class.

Since the plane had passed over Winnipeg he'd been looking at the prairie far below. The straight lines of the roads, the chequerboard grain fields, the innumerable sloughs that looked like tiny mud-holes. In the past forty years he'd flown thousands of miles in different parts of the world, but he had never seen anything like the land below him now. And it was his land; he'd been born here, grown up, felt pain and horrible frustration, and, yes, love.

Why had he never been back? And, more to the point, why was he coming back now for this family reunion? Family. His family. But he'd never really felt a part of it, any more than he'd felt at home on the prairies in the desolate thirties.

As the plane began its descent, details of the land became more clear. Railway lines, tiny towns, grain elevators, farmsteads surrounded by shelter belts of box elder, caragana, and poplar trees, little patches of green on the flat land. Oh, he remembered those farms, all right.

The land had changed since 1937, when he'd left this place for good. And his family. Great changes in forty-three years, from abject poverty to prosperity. The province, too, once the poorest in Canada, was now one of the more prosperous.

As the plane flew lower, Hugh could see the city and the wide Saskatchewan River winding through it, the six bridges, the university buildings perched on the bank. The airport was on the edge of town.

And then he was a twelve-year-old boy again, riding his bike out Avenue A to the old airport with its rickety sheds to see the marvel of the world, an air show. He remembered the thrill of watching the Gypsy Moths looping high above as people stood beside their cars, gaping in sheer wonder.

The big jet made a smooth landing and taxied up to the small new terminal building. As the plane came to a stop the pretty stewardess helped Hugh with his carry-on luggage and smiled pleasantly at him.

"Goodbye, sir. Have a good day." Gone, just like that, as Elaine had gone forty-three years earlier.

He walked out the door and into the tunnel that led to the terminal. He emerged into a hallway and saw a stout man, prosperous, well dressed but still a little sloppy-looking in his expensive clothes. The man rushed forward, threw a beefy arm around Hugh's shoulder.

"Squirt, I'd know you anywhere!"

"Squirt." Nobody had called him that in years. He was back, all right.

"How the hell are you, boy?" his brother Tom shouted, pounding him on the back. "Jesus but you're skinny!"

"That's more than I can say for you, Tom. You look fat and prosperous."

"Oh, I've done all right. Yeah, for a farm boy with no

education, I haven't done bad at all. Come on, let me take that bag. I wasn't supposed to be up here, but I can always pull a few strings." He laughed a good-natured laugh. "I got a surprise for you, little brother."

No matter what he'd done, what fame he'd achieved, to Tom he'd always be little brother.

Tom led the way, weaving between the crowds of people, down the escalator, and into a plush waiting room with padded chairs and round glass tables.

"There she is," Tom said, "over there. She hasn't seen you yet."

Hugh looked where his brother pointed and there, sitting prim and straight as always, was a woman who seemed of uncertain age, smartly dressed, reading a magazine.

"Ma, look who's here," Tom boomed as they approached. "The long-lost has returned."

Martha Windmar got to her feet and Hugh saw signs of her eighty-seven years.

"Hughie," she said softly. "It really is you. You've come home at last!"

Tears glistened in her eyes. Hugh remembered there'd been tears there when he got on the train to go east so many years ago. He put his arm around her.

"Yeah, Ma, it's really me." He kissed her cheek and felt the wrinkles under the make-up. Then he stepped back. "Ma, you still look great."

"Fiddlesticks, I'm an old lady." But he could see she was pleased. Always a woman with class.

"Where's Dad?" he asked.

"Your father? Well, he's where he always is at this time of day. Down at the brokerage office, watching himself get richer by the minute."

"Good for him. God knows he was poor long enough."

"Now that's the truth," Tom boomed. "But look at us now, eh? The Windmars have done all right. You the world's most famous playwright. Gwen – Jesus, that woman, all those books she writes, and lectures. And I used to wipe her bottom!"

"Tom, really," Martha admonished mildly. She never had reconciled herself to her oldest son's rough language, but she'd long since stopped worrying about it.

"You haven't done so badly yourself," Hugh said.

"Nope, by God, I haven't and that's for damned sure!"

"Didn't I hear you were mayor of the city?"

"Two terms. Put this burg on its feet. Then I quit. Sold the business and now I'm travelling around the province talking to Rotarians, trying to sell them on free trade with the United States."

"Haven't you ever thought of retiring?"

"Retiring? What's that? Let's go."

He led the way through the terminal to the baggage counter, then outside to his new Cadillac, parked in front of the terminal doors.

"Isn't it illegal to park here?" Hugh asked.

"Not if you've got pull. Thanks, Harry," he said to the policeman whose job it was to prevent people from parking there.

"Welcome, Mr. Windmar," the cop said with a grin.

"Who else is coming?" Hugh asked as Tom manoeuvred the car onto the highway.

"Whole damned shooting match," Tom said. "Gwen flew in from New York, where she's been at some conference. Olive met her."

Olive and Gwen. The two sisters had never gotten along. Hugh wondered how the visit would work out.

"Gwen's been home a few times, hasn't she?" Hugh asked his mother.

"A lot oftener than you have, Hughie. Why did you never come back?"

"Too busy, I guess. Travelling, writing, openings. It eats up your time. I always meant to." He was lying; he had never wanted to come back to Saskatoon. The place reminded him of humiliation and frustration.

"Well, you're home now, anyway. I hope you can stay awhile."

"Olive still on the ranch?" Hugh asked.

"Yep," Tom said. "Down in the Cypress Hills." He said it with the exaggerated drawl he always used when he named the ranching country. "Still married to Clayton, too, of course."

"Clayton's not coming, is he?"

"Nope. No spouses or kids in on this deal. Just the Windmar kids. We can take off the gloves and have at it."

"God, I hope not. And Shawn?"

"Shawn, the baby of the family. Lucky bugger. Never knew any of the bad times – Depression, war. He's an engineer now, lives in Vancouver. Yeah, he's here. Plane got in late last night. I met him."

Just like always, Hugh thought. Tom, the take-over guy. Where would this family have been without him?

There was one they didn't mention. Alvin, Martha's favourite. Glancing at his mother in the back seat, Hugh guessed she was thinking of her lost son. Probably never stopped thinking of him.

The car swung onto Circle Drive, which goes around the city.

"Isn't this a little out of the way?" Hugh asked.

"Ah, I just want to show you some of the things been happening to our fair city since you left. Wait till you see the new subdivisions out Eighth Street."

"Eighth Street. You mean out east where we used to go to snare gophers?"

"Brother, are you behind the times. All built up now, with subdivisions clear to Sutherland. I tell you, this is the fastest-growing city in Canada. We got shopping malls you wouldn't believe."

Hugh was about to mention the Eaton Centre in Toronto, but he stopped, remembering that Toronto was a dirty word to most westerners.

"It sure has changed," was all he said. Then he asked, "Ma, you're still in the house on River Crescent, aren't you?"

"Oh dear, yes. It's far too big for us, of course. But Will could never give up that house. It means so much to him.

There'll be plenty of room for you all to stay there."

"Yeah, plenty of room everywhere," Tom added. "Hell, we could put up half a dozen in our house, now that the kids have all moved out."

"How are they doing, your kids?" Hugh asked.

"Fine, fine. Spread all over hell's half acre. I got an even dozen grandkids, and two greats. Prolific family. All but Gwen and you, you bugger."

Here it comes, Hugh thought. Questions, suggestions, criticisms. Won't be long before we're at it. Families. The only people in the world who feel they have a right to take liberties. Well, he'd get the hell out as fast as he could. But first there was one thing he had to take care of. One big question he must answer.

When they stopped in front of the house on River Crescent, Hugh helped Martha from the back seat and then stood staring. The stone wall along the front of the property, the huge, landscaped lawns, the house itself, stone and brick with immense windows facing the river: everything oozed wealth and the good life.

"Quite a change from the shack you were in when I left," he muttered.

Tom laughed and slapped him on the back. "Lot of changes since you were here. You know, having dough is a lot more fun."

Chapter Two

Hugh Windmar sat in his father's comfortable leather chair in the living room of the big house. Through the picture window he could see, across the street, the bank of the Saskatchewan River and the scrub birch and chokecherry bushes that fringed the road. Through the trees he caught a glimpse of the broad, sluggish river; in the distance was downtown Saskatoon.

Hugh's brothers and sisters were reminiscing about childhood days, but Hugh wasn't listening. He was thinking bitter thoughts.

What a fool he'd been to allow Gwen to talk him into coming back. Family reunion, what was the point of it? His parents, although old, weren't sick. He had left his comfortable apartment in Toronto and his comfortable mistress to come to this godforsaken place. Even the weather wasn't decent; it was hot and windy. Typical. And these people: strangers, really. He'd never had much to do with them, except for Tom, and that had been a lousy relationship, Tom leading and he following. And Alvin. Well, he wasn't going to think of Alvin after shutting him out of his mind for thirty-eight years. As for Shawn, he'd been a mere toddler when Hugh left the province.

He had to admit that coming back after forty-three years hadn't been all Gwen's doing. For all those years, the place had bugged him. The rotten Depression had stolen ten years from his life – and there was Elaine. "Elaine the fair, Elaine the lovable," he had called her during those mad, lusty, excruciating days and nights he'd courted her, mostly on long walks along the railroad tracks that fall and winter.

Twenty-two years old. God, that was forty-three years ago! There had been scarcely a moment in all those years that she'd been out of his mind.

"Day-dreaming, brother?" His sister Olive broke in on his thoughts as she lit another cigarette. Olive, a real daughter of the prairies, just as Tom was a real westerner. She seemed happy enough with all her kids and grandchildren. Her husband, Clayton, was successful, well known as head of the Cattlemen's Association. Of course he was rarely home.

"No, sister dear, I was just thinking."

"About Ontario probably. Honest to God, I don't see how you can live in that smug, self-satisfied place!"

"I think smug and self-satisfied are the same thing," Gwendolyn put in.

"Pardon me for living," replied Olive.

Tom took a sip of his Scotch and grinned at his sister.

"You know, Gwen baby," he said, "you got to make allowances for us western slobs. We ain't never had the advantages of a Ph.D. or travelling all over the world nor nothing." He grinned devilishly at the effect his bad grammar had on his sister. "Now you take me. I never made it out of public school, never learned no Latin, but I've done all right."

"Indeed you have," Gwen said. "Past president of just about everything in Saskatchewan, as well as being mayor emeritus of this city. But you know, you've been lucky - I mean having all that drive and energy. Compared with education, drive and energy will win out any time."

"You slobbered a bibful there, sister."

"Well, yes," Hugh said. "Here we are, and we all made it. During the Depression I wouldn't have given a nickel for any of our chances."

"All except Alvin," Olive said quietly. She had an abrasive, pugnacious side, but she could also be very gentle.

"Yeah, the original hard-luck kid," Tom said fondly. "Never got a decent break in his life."

The others sat silent, thinking of their dead brother.

"I know Mother says a prayer for him every night," Gwen

said. "And she reads his poems regularly."

"Yeah, those poems of his. I often wonder how a person like Alvin could have been born into this family of bozos," Olive said.

"Speak for yourself there," Hugh bristled. "We all write the scripts for our own lives. Alvin just wrote a lousy script."

"Bulll-sheeit!" Tom exploded, his grin gone. "Lots of people helped him write that damned script, as you call it. Don't give us any of that existentialist crap!"

Gwen's eyebrows lifted. Tom never ceased to surprise her.

"Especially that girl," Olive said, furtively wiping her eyes. "She killed him. I'll always believe that."

"Nonsense. She did what she did for her own selfish reasons. Don't we all do that?" Gwen asked.

"Like hell we do," Shawn burst out. "Oh, I know you had it bad, and I didn't. But that's all past. It's the future we have to fight for, or we'll all end up like Alvin, and damned soon – with super-powers fighting like kids and eager to push the button and blow us all to hell!" He got up from his chair and faced them. "Don't you see, unless we do something there won't be any future for us or our kids or – "

"I wonder where Mother is," Gwen interrupted, hoping to avert an argument.

"Ma?" Tom took it up. "She had a hair appointment."

"At her age?" Hugh snorted.

"You don't know much about women, brother dear," Olive said. "Never did. Age has got nothing to do with it. And the older she gets the more important a woman's hair becomes to her."

"Yeah, and you gotta admit there aren't many ninety-year-old dames look as good as Ma does."

"She's not ninety," Olive said. "She was born in 1893 and that makes her only eighty-seven!"

"Sure, look at Lillian Gish and Ruth Gordon, still acting," Hugh mused.

"Did you ever meet either of them?" Tom asked. He was

fascinated by his brother's success.

"Ruth Gordon was in my first Broadway play."

"Is that a fact? And Lillian Gish. I remember her in the movies. Sure had a crush on that one."

"You had a crush on every pretty girl you ever saw," Olive said.

"Just liked to spread it around, sister. Nothing selfish about me."

"That's no way to talk," Olive scolded, looking pointedly at her sister.

Hugh noticed the look. Olive had always implied that Gwen had never had a sex life. It was only partly true. A precocious child with an inordinately high intelligence, Gwen had been a whiz at school. Always first in her class, absorbing knowledge as a sponge absorbs water. Pushed from grade to grade, until she finished high school early and went on to university. She continued to distinguish herself until she had three doctorates, in anthropology, the social sciences, and psychology. Then she began writing books and lecturing, and her reputation extended far beyond Canada and North America.

Now she was trying to learn about their family. She'd told Hugh that she'd searched the family tree as far back as she could, until it was lost in the mists of Northern Ireland. Now she was setting her parents' story on tape, before it was too late.

"Where has Dad got himself to?" Shawn wanted to know. "All the way from Vancouver I come to be with them, and I've hardly even seen Dad."

"Well, if you want to be with the old man," Tom said, "just take your butt down to Second Avenue and the brokerage office of Smithson and Grauch. He'll be there, smoking his cigar and watching the big board."

"Yeah, ever since he got rich all he thinks of is making more money. You'd think he'd have enough," Shawn said.

"There is never enough," Hugh said. "Especially if you've once been as poor as he was. Making marmalade in the kitchen and Alvin and I peddling it door to door. God, the humiliation. That's the worst thing about poverty, the humiliation!"

"Nope." Tom grinned. "It's putting cardboard in the soles of your shoes so you won't wear out your socks."

"Here we go," Shawn burst out. "Hardships, ruddy hardships. Once you get talking about hardships . . . God!"

"You Yuppies can just thank your lucky stars you never had any to remember," Olive said.

"I feel deprived. No hardships to talk about. No Depression stories, no war stories. It wasn't my fault Dad struck it rich. I was five years old when the war began. After that there were no hardships."

"For you or this wretched province," Hugh said. "Let's hear it for Hitler. He saved us all. Oh, to hell with it." He stood up. "Tom, where can I rent a car?"

"Planning a little trip? I'll take you anywhere you want to go."

"No, thanks. This trip I have to take alone."

"Where you going?"

"Oh, just out in the country. It looks so different now. Last time I saw it there was nothing but blowing dust and grasshoppers chewing up half-dead crops."

"You'll see a big difference now, brother," Tom said with enthusiasm. "I could show you some great fields of rape, all yellow. Man, it's pretty."

"Rape?"

"Yeah, that's what a lot of the farmers are growing now. Land of rape and honey, old Dief used to call it. When do you want to go?"

"Well, I thought. . . ."

"I get it. Like Garbo, you 'want to be alone.' Well, to hell with rented cars, take the Buick. It's just sitting there in the garage."

Hugh looked at him. "You always were the most generous bastard I ever knew. I remember the first time you loaned me your car. . . ."

"The old Buick coupe back in the thirties, for your first big date."

"Yeah, what a disaster."

"Nuff said. When do you want to go?"

"I'm not sure. One of these days, before I leave. Right now I'd like to take a walk. Want to come?"

"Damn betcha. Lead on, Macduff."

"I think I know where Hugh wants to go in the country," Olive said after the brothers had left.

"Where?" Gwen asked.

"To Harman."

"You mean where he used to teach?"

"Yep. I have a feeling he's got some unfinished business in that neck of the woods."

Chapter Three

"I can't figure out what keeps the old bugger going," Tom said fondly, referring to his father. Tom and Hugh had just returned from their walk on which Tom had told his brother about the deteriorating condition of their parents' health. Now they were back in the living room with the rest of the family.

Olive laughed, both at Tom's crudity and her sister's reaction to it. "What keeps him going is good food, exercise, and clean living."

"Yeah," Tom said. "Smokes half a dozen cigars a day, eats gobs of fried foods, white bread, and white sugar, never took a vitamin pill in his life, drinks good Scotch every day, and all the exercise he gets is lifting his arse out of the chair in the brokerage office downtown and getting into the car. He even has a chauffeur to drive him."

"It's heredity and natural selection," Gwendolyn explained. "Survival of the fittest. All the weak ones were weeded out of that strain in Northern Ireland or on the boat coming over. His grandfather was the sole survivor of eight family members who sailed from Ireland in 1846."

"You should write a book about it," Tom said.

"I'm thinking of that. So far my notes are in a rather disorganized state. But I think Father's flair for economics and investments comes naturally, too - he just didn't have a chance to exercise it until after the war. Another member of the family became very rich in the lumber trade in Ontario."

"Well, I'm damned," Tom said. "Always wondered where his knack for business came from."

"Some flair," Hugh said. "They strike oil on your farm and you just happen to own the mineral rights. Pure luck."

"Call it chance," his sister corrected. "But the important thing is what he did with the money once he got it."

"Hey," Shawn said. He'd been sitting quietly, half listening to the others while he thumbed through the latest issue of *Harrowsmith*. "I'd sure like to visit the old homestead. We could drive out there."

"Excellent idea," Gwen agreed. "I'm sure Father and Mother would like to go."

"Don't kid yourself," Tom said. "Ma's got no great love for that place. Stands to reason. Foxy gal from Toron-bloody-to coming out to this godforsaken country."

"Where is it, anyway?" Shawn asked. "I've often wondered."

"West of here," Tom explained. "Not far from the Alberta border. Town of Edenvale. Wasn't more than a hamlet when we were there, but you should see it now. Good-sized town, full of oil money."

"What's on the old farm?" Shawn asked.

"Not a damned thing. I went out that way a couple of times the year I was travelling for that damned cement company." He made a face at the memory.

"Who owns the place?"

"Guess the oil company still does, though there's no more oil."

"Wonder what they'd want for it?" Shawn was thinking out loud.

"Surely you're not thinking of moving back to Saskatchewan?" Hugh asked.

"What's wrong with Saskatchewan?" Olive flared.

"What's right with it, you mean."

"Just because you had such a hard time here, you don't need to take that attitude. After all, that was the Depression. We all had a hard time!"

"I agree," Gwen said.

"Land's mighty expensive now," Tom said to change the subject.

"Yeah, I suppose so," Shawn replied. "But maybe a person could get hold of some. How about in one of these deserted towns I hear about?"

"Maybe. Mighty damned lonely, though. You figuring to move Alice and the kids out here?"

"I'd like to live off the land as much as possible," Shawn said, his eyes shining with enthusiasm. "You know, grow a big garden, raise chickens, rabbits, have a cow, maybe a pig or two."

"Self-sufficient," Gwen said.

"Yeah. Much as possible. Then when the big bang comes and cities like Ottawa and Toronto and the rest are flattened, a person might have a chance to save himself and his kids away out here."

"Don't you just love it?" Olive scoffed. " 'Away out here.' We call Toronto and Ottawa 'away out there.' "

"Oh, you know what I mean."

"Damn betcha," Tom said. "I got a couple hundred acres out there at Pickerel Lake. Build a house on a piece of that, if you want. No charge. I could show you a thing or two about farming."

"Yeah, I guess you could all right." Shawn's enthusiasm was gone.

"Here's Father," Gwen said, glancing out the big front window at William Henry, who had started up the walk then stopped to inspect his shrubs. "My goodness, but he does have a firm step for a man of eighty-eight."

"Yep," Olive agreed proudly. "Still got that confident western-farmer stride."

"He does that," Tom said with genuine admiration. "I can still see him striding across the pasture after that old bull we used to have. Mean bastard he was. One day he turned on the old man."

"What happened?" Shawn asked.

"Well, I was tagging along behind him the way I usually did. Old Major was in the mood, as we say. A cow was coming into heat and I guess he could smell her. He had horns about a foot long, and sharp. Ma always wanted Dad to cut the horns off that bull, but he wouldn't. Said it would spoil his looks. Well, that old bugger put his head down and hooked at Dad. The old man saw it coming and turned just in time. If he hadn't, you girls'd never have been born. Anyway, the horn caught him on the outside of the thigh instead of the crotch."

"What happened then?" Shawn asked.

"Well, Dad let out the damnedest shout you ever heard and hit that bull on the nose with his fist. The old man could hit. I saw him knock a hired man flat once. Old Major just shook his head and backed off. Somehow Dad managed to get himself over the fence, and me under it. God, I'll never forget that."

"Go on," Gwen urged.

"Well, we were about half a mile from the house and Dad bleeding like a stuck pig. He pulled his big red handkerchief from his overall pocket and bound it around his thigh. Then he took my handkerchief and shoved it into the hole. And then, by Jesus, he walked that half mile home – with a little help from me."

Tom wiped his eyes and went on.

"We didn't have a phone. There was no doctor in Edenvale. We were on our own. Ma poured iodine into the wound. We always kept a big bottle of iodine. Then she wrapped it up. No tetanus shots, no stitches. He was out in the field in a couple of days. Had to be. The weather was right for seeding and he had to get the wheat into the ground. Every night Ma dressed that wound and put poultices on it. If he'd got blood poisoning he'd have been a goner. I stayed out of school and helped him." Tom threw back his head and laughed. "Yeah, and old Miss Thompson, she raised hell. But I was no good in school. Hugh was the smart one. Just as well, because he was never much use around the farm."

Hugh coloured slightly, started to say something then stopped. In his mind he said, Yes, you bastard, you could always work better than I could and play baseball and hockey better and screw the girls better. Damn, why did

I ever let myself get talked into coming to this reunion?

William Henry came into the room. He was tall and lean with a good head of hair.

"Well, now," he said with a chuckle. "All the children here, I see." He walked over to Hugh and took his hand. "Even you, son. A sight for sore eyes if I ever saw one. You've been away quite some time."

Hugh stood holding his father's hand, the hand of an old man. "Too long, I'm afraid," he said.

"Ah pshaw. You've been busy like the rest of us. Living your own life in your own way. Anyway, you're here now. Yes, yes indeed. Well . . ."

"Dad, how would you like to go for a ride in the country?" Shawn asked. "I'd sure like to see – "

"Country, eh?" his dad interrupted. "By God, I haven't been out in the country for a long time. Must be years."

"We were wondering if you and Mother might like to drive out to the old homestead," Gwen said.

William Henry laughed. "The old homestead! What for? Nothing there but some broken-down oil rigs and the bald-headed prairie."

"We were just talking about it," Olive said. "Tom told us the story about the bull."

"Bull? What bull?"

"Old Major," Tom said. "Time he hooked you in the thigh."

"Oh yes, yes. I mind that all right. Miserable old bastard he was. I've still got the scar on my thigh. If Tom hadn't been along I'd have never made it home. But he was and I did." He grinned at the memory. "That's not the only close call I had out there."

"What else?" Gwen asked.

"Worst was when I caught the sleeve of my coat in the chopper. Danged near pulled me in, but I managed to yank the buttons off and get out of the coat. Farm's a danged dangerous place to be. But we had a lot of fun."

"Fun?" Hugh scoffed. "Doesn't sound like much fun, living in a two-room shack, working from sun-up to dark. . . ."

"Two-room shack's all right if you got a good person to share it with you. By the way, where is my bride?"

"At the hairdresser's," Gwen told him.

"Yeah. Got to keep looking pretty. Always was the prettiest thing I ever saw, and the smartest, too. I tell you they don't make them any better than your Ma."

"We all agree with you there," Gwen said. "We were most fortunate in our parents."

"Yes, yes, and us in our children." William Henry was obviously flustered at such talk. "Well, if you will excuse me for a while, I've got some paperwork to do and some phone calls to make."

"Stock market kicking up?" Hugh asked.

"Always, always. Got to watch it like a hawk. I tell you, if you don't . . . but enough of that. I'll only be a little while. Help yourself to anything you want." He left the room.

"Still the same," Olive mused. "Soon as you get near anything personal he shies off."

"It's a generation thing," Gwen explained. "Victorians were very reserved and – "

"Yeah, yeah, we know," Olive cut in. "I'm going downtown to do some shopping, Gwen. Want to come with me?"

"No, I think I'll stay here. I have some letters to write and I'd like to talk to Father."

Chapter Four

"This damned fool family reunion is a colossal mistake," Hugh Windmar said. He looked at his brothers and sisters, seated in comfortable lawn chairs in the spacious yard of William Henry's house. It was a beautiful yard, with curving flower beds and ornamental shrubs.

The whole scene reeked of prosperity and contentment. Tom reclined on a wooden chaise longue well padded with cushions. He wore an expensive sport shirt and hundred-and-fifty-dollar slacks. He'd kicked off his expensive loafers and was wiggling his toes. Beside him on a ceramic table was a tall glass of Scotch and soda.

"How so, brother?" he asked, more serious than usual. "You've only been here one day. How can you say that?"

"Yeah, what the hell do you mean?" Olive said. Her blouse was open at the neck and her flared skirt covered her chair. In deference to the occasion she'd forgone her usual jeans.

Gwen was more formal, in a trim, pleated summer dress. Shawn, bored out of his skull, sat cross-legged on the grass with a can of beer in his hand. He wore shorts and no shoes. Hugh Windmar was dressed like Tom, but on his trim figure the clothes looked good.

"Well, look at us, for Christ's sake, sitting here like a group at a Rotarian picnic with nothing to talk about. Hell, we never had anything to talk about when we all lived at home, except to fight. We're all different. We lead different lives, have different thoughts, prejudices. I say let's forget the whole damned thing and go our separate ways."

"Now, just a damned minute there," Tom said. "So we're

a little different. Okay, but we're a family. We all came from the same people. Damned good people, too, if you ask me."

Olive and Gwen were quiet, a little apprehensive, knowing the explosive propensities of their brothers' tempers.

"We're all here," Tom went on. "For the first time in years and for damned sure the last time. Ma and Dad haven't long to live – they're old, damn it. We're all old, for that matter. We can stick it out for a week. Won't kill us."

"What in hell are we going to do?" Hugh asked.

"I have a suggestion," Gwen offered. "It's a game psychologists use to solve problems."

"Here we go with the psychology crap," Olive said.

"You know what they say," Shawn put in. "Anybody who goes to a psychiatrist should have his head read."

"Old joke," Tom said, "and not very funny."

"Sorry, I was just trying to – "

"Shut up. What's this game you eggheads play?" Tom asked.

"Well, it's called Remembering. Each one of us remembers something from our childhood and tells it."

"Sounds like a dumb game," Shawn said.

"I warned you," Tom said. "You're not too big for me to clobber."

"We're off to a good start," Hugh said. "A good knock-down, drag-out fight might clear the air."

"What are we going to remember?" Olive asked uneasily. "Good things or bad things?"

"Both. Just whatever comes into your head."

"The most dangerous game," Hugh said.

Olive got out of her lawn chair and came over to Hugh. "It is, eh? Well, I'd like to hear about what happened to you out there in Harman. I know something happened. But what? Was there a girl? There was a girl, wasn't there?"

"A girl? Dozens of them. Place was a veritable Hollywood full of starlets. All ripe for the picking."

"One special girl?"

One girl, Hugh thought. Yes, there was one girl. A girl he loved and betrayed. He wasn't ready to talk about that.

"No special girl," he lied.

"Oh, you're no fun," his sister said, going back to her chair.

"I told you it wouldn't work."

"I remember one," Tom said, laughing. "But I warn you, it's pretty raunchy. Don't know if you can take it."

"We're all adults here," Gwen said. "No puritans among us, and after all, this is 1980, when just about everything goes, in the movies, on television, anywhere."

"It's really pretty funny," Tom said. "And I've never told anyone about it."

"Well, you've got my interest, brother," Olive said.

"I trust it doesn't deal with incest," Shawn quipped.

"You're close. Happened on the homestead when I was still a kid, but feeling my oats. Spring. You know what spring is like on the farm. Every living thing - cats, chickens, horses, pigs - all horny as hell."

"And people," Hugh said, remembering.

"Oh, yeah, people. I was only a kid but I was a horny little bugger."

"Was?" Olive said.

Tom ignored her. "It was one of those warm spring mornings, when the snow is all gone and the manure pile beside the barn is thawing out and things are just beginning to grow. Crocuses on the hills. Remember the crocuses on the hills? It was warm and rather sultry. Whole family had gone to church in town, drove there in the old Model T. First time Dad had it out after the winter, I remember. But I didn't go to church with the rest. Made up some story about not feeling well. Truth is I was too restless to sit still that long."

"And horny," Shawn said.

Tom glared at Shawn and continued with his story.

"We had a lot of chickens then and they were wandering about the barnyard, pecking at whatever they could find, bugs, frogs, grasshopper nymphs, anything. In and out of the barn where there were always some oats spilled on the floor.

"Suddenly I heard the damnedest racket coming from the barn. I went up to the door and sort of sneaked in. And there was our hired man, Nick. Remember him? The one with the squint. You used to imitate him, Hugh. Funniest thing."

"What was Nick doing?" Olive said. "Or dare I ask?"

"He was screwing a hen."

"Sodomizing it?" Gwen asked.

"That too. And that hen was squawking and there were feathers and blood all over the place. When he finished he wrung its neck and threw it onto the manure pile and pushed a forkful of straw over it. Then he went out of the barn. He didn't see me."

"What a revolting story!" Olive said.

"Where's the funny part?" Shawn asked.

Tom laughed. "Well, I thought that it was quite a good idea. By this time I was pretty worked up, if you know what I mean. So I decided to catch me a hen."

"Tom! You didn't!" Gwen said.

"I tried. Picked out a nice plump hen and took after her. But they can run. This one went all around the barnyard with me after it and old Gyp after me. I nearly caught it a couple of times but just missed. Then it flew over the fence into the pigpen, and me after it. Caught my foot on the fence and fell on my face in all that pig shit. Well, that kind of cooled my ardour, as they say, but I had a problem. How was I going to explain the mess I was in when the folks got home from church?"

"You'd think of a way," Hugh said.

Tom smiled. "I was wearing my overalls and an old shirt. I took them off and put them in the horse trough and scrubbed them good and hung them on a fence to dry. Then, you remember that shower Dad rigged up in an old granary? It was a barrel set up on a stand with a pipe coming down. Homemade shower. He'd use it when he came in from the field all dust and sweat. So I filled the barrel and gave myself a shower, cold but effective. Then I went into the house and put on my Sunday suit. When the folks came home I told Ma I thought that since it was Sunday I should dress up. She was pleased."

There was some laughter.

"Well," Gwen said, "I've heard of a lot of different first sexual experiences, but never one quite like that."

"Oh, that wasn't the first," Tom said. "Remember that little red-head in grade six? Well. . . ."

"I think we've heard enough," Olive said.

Tom was still laughing. He wiped his eyes with a handkerchief. "Okay, that's my story. Who's next?"

"How about you, Shawn?" Hugh asked. "You're so much younger than the rest of us – we know very little about your life."

"Yes," Gwen said. "We had the thirties and the war but we missed the drug culture and all the rest that happened in the sixties."

Shawn stood up, walked to the border of the lawn, and picked one of Martha's roses. "Yeah, the sixties. Seems like such a long time ago. Funny time. Don't know what got into everybody. Maybe we just had too much."

"Couldn't stand prosperity," Tom said.

"Something like that. One thing for sure, we didn't want to settle down, get into some big corporation with a good pension plan. No, we wanted something else. I had been out of university for a few years and had a good job. Jobs were plentiful then. If you didn't like your job or just wanted a holiday you took off. Could always get another."

"Did you try drugs?" Hugh asked.

"Oh, I smoked a bit. Who didn't? Quite a bit, in fact. But I gradually gave it up. Never got into the hard stuff. Yeah, it was some time." He picked the petals from the rose one by one. "Hitch-hiking was the thing."

"Did you hitch-hike?"

"Yeah, me and Jinny Wong. Now there was a girl. Father was a doctor, straight-laced as they come. Boy, did he raise a fuss when Jinny said we were going. Threatened to have me thrown in jail. But Jinny took care of that. She was nineteen and he couldn't do a thing. So we got our stuff together and away we went, riding on the thumb."

"What was it like?" Olive asked.

"Hell. Pure unadulterated hell. I know you guys had some rough times, but have you ever stood on the side of a highway a thousand miles from home in the rain, or the blazing sun, and had cars - thousands of cars - pass you by? That is the worst thing I can think of." He paused, remembering. "Do you know that one old bastard tried to kill us? Fact. Drove his big car over on the shoulder straight at us. We thought he was going to stop and pick us up. But he came straight at us!"

"What happened?"

"I grabbed Jinny just in time and we hit the ditch."

"Where did this happen?" Tom asked.

"On that straight stretch of road between Regina and Moose Jaw. God, I'll never forget it. I was for going home, but Jinny wouldn't hear of it. Lot of spunk, that girl."

"What happened to her?"

"Married a Chinese doctor. Did I tell you she was Chinese? Very traditional family. Her father. You know he didn't even admit that I existed? I was a non-person to him. But that Jinny. Wow!"

"So?" Hugh asked.

"That's all. We finally took a bus home. In British Columbia it rained steadily for a week. And that was that. End of adventure. End of story." He stood looking at the remains of the rose in his hand. "So now I'm a nice respectable engineer with a good wife and a family and a job with all the medical benefits and a good pension plan, everything a good Canadian Yuppie could want." He looked around at his brothers and sisters. "And I hate it. Ah, to hell with it."

The others were silent, thinking their own thoughts.

"Who's next?" Tom finally said.

Gwen cleared her throat. "I have one." She looked at Olive. "It goes back to high-school days, and a dance."

Olive sprang to her feet. "You're not going to tell that!" she shouted. "Don't you dare!" She ran into the house.

"I think I've had enough of these true confessions," Tom said. "Besides, if I don't get my ass out of here my wife will leave me." He went into the house.

"Me, too," Shawn said. "I'm going in to see if I can't convince Dad to take me out to the old homestead." He followed his brother.

"So that leaves you and me." Hugh got out of his chair and stood in front of Gwen. "Okay, sister, what's this thing between you and Olive?"

"Why nothing." But she wasn't looking at him.

"Don't give me that. I know better. Out with it."

"You promise you won't use it in a play or anything?"

"Word of honour."

"Well, it goes back to when we were both in high school. It's the reason she hates me."

"Come now, isn't that a bit strong? What did you do to her?"

"It's what she did to me. We always hate those we have wronged. Why do you think the whites hate the blacks?"

"Yeah, hate is a more pleasant emotion than guilt."

"So the English hate the Irish, the Germans hate the Jews, the Turks hate the Armenians, we hate the Indians and Olive hates me."

"What did Olive ever do to you?"

"Stole my boyfriend. At least she thinks she did, and that amounts to the same thing."

"You mean her husband Clayton?"

"The very same. I think I loved Clayton."

"My God. I never knew."

"Nobody did."

"That's the trouble with reunions. Open old wounds."

"I hope not, since it was my idea."

"I give us another two days and we'll be at each other's

throats. All the old resentments will flare up. We'll fight just as we did as kids. What a crazy family." He shook his head sadly.

"Not crazy, just different. Evenly divided between the slobs and the intellectuals. If we didn't have the same parents and live in the same house, we would probably never have anything to do with each other. But our forced association was good for all of us."

"Oh, sure."

"What do you think goaded me into getting all those degrees? Olive, that's what."

"Tell me about Clayton."

"Only if you promise not to use the story in one of your plays."

"Okay. Not directly, anyway."

"Well, it happened when we were both going to Gardner Collegiate. Even though we were practically the same age, we were vastly different. Olive could hang by her knees from the swing bar and I never could. She could run faster, jump higher, and see better. In grades one and two, they thought I was slightly retarded. I just couldn't see the damned blackboard well enough to know what was going on. Then they instituted this eye-examination program and discovered I was terribly short-sighted."

"I wonder how many rural kids are branded as dumb because they can't see."

"Quite a few, I suspect. Anyway, those glasses changed my life in more ways than one. I began to love school, but the glasses restricted me on the playground and affected my social life. So I studied harder and did better in school. Do you know boys are afraid of bright girls?"

"I always was. But you were so damned pretty."

"Well, thanks. On one date I tried taking off my glasses. Like Marilyn Monroe in *How to Marry a Millionaire*." Gwen laughed. "I ran into things and couldn't see the movie, and when we went to eat afterwards at the Palace of Sweets I just said I'd have whatever Herb ordered. It was a tuna-salad sandwich – and I hate tuna salad. I never tried that again.

"It's funny. I'll swear Olive is just as bright as I am. That 'western slob' stuff is just a pose. But when she was out playing with the boys during those delightful spring evenings, I was inside studying. So I skipped a couple of grades in public school and got ahead of her. She was always on the basketball team and the softball team and she developed earlier. Had good breasts before she left grade eight, while I was flat as a board."

"Sounds a lot like Tom and me."

"Tom had big breasts?"

"No, but he could do everything better than I could, except school work. Thank God for school."

"I agree. Anyway, we were different, and Mother was no help. Always trying to get me to go out more and Olive to stay in more. And of course we were broke. If it hadn't been for the money you sent me, I wouldn't have been able to pay my student-council fees in high school. You were teaching at Harman then. Remember?"

Hugh wasn't listening. He was back in Harman, where as a mere nineteen-year-old he'd taken over the principalship of a three-room continuation school. And Elaine. "Elaine the fair, Elaine the lovable." Tennyson's poetry, and Shelley and Keats. How he'd loved to read it to his senior class. That damned Depression. It had blighted his life.

"Did you hate it as much as I did? The Depression?" he asked.

"Not really. Just after I got out of high school the war had started and the Depression was over, so I could go to university. Thank God for the war. But even in high school it wasn't so bad for me. Mother made all our clothes, and we had the prettiest dresses in school. But she did one terrible thing."

"What was that?"

"Well, it was when we were in high school. There was a big dance at the school, an annual affair called the Alumni

Dance. You had to get a date from a senior student or an alumnus to go. It was very fancy, with Guy Watkins and his Art Harmony Seven providing the music and all the girls in long gowns. The social event of the year. Mother made our party dresses. Identical. White organdy with mauve flowers and frills around the bottom and over the shoulders, low-cut in front and lower in the back. I guess she got a bargain on the cloth and that's why she made them the same. I was so excited about that dance!"

"And Clayton?"

"Oh, yes, Clayton. A good student and rather shy. We used to walk home from school together. He sold his bike to get the ten dollars to buy the dance tickets and a corsage – a corsage was a must – and he invited me to go with him. Oh, my!"

"Did you wear your glasses to the dance?"

"Oh, yes, but Clayton didn't wear his. He was short-sighted, too, not nearly as bad as I, but bad enough. Well, Olive had a date for the dance, of course. I was in seventh heaven, as they say. My big night. Clayton came to get me in a taxi! Olive's date fetched her in his father's car.

"I remember that auditorium. Decorated with streamers and stars and bells, all in the school colours, light blue and dark. And the orchestra on the stage. It was very formal and nice, with a promenade to begin with, and the principal and his wife and all the teachers in formal dress. Clayton and I had the first dance, but he wasn't a very good dancer, at least with me he wasn't. But I put his name down on my program for the third, sixth, ninth, and last dance, which was the rule."

"And the rest of the dances?"

"Oh, I had no trouble filling up my card. I was no wallflower. And then, as the music was beginning for the third dance, Olive and I happened to be standing together when Clayton came up for his dance. We were about the same height and wearing identical dresses and that damned short-sighted Clayton took her instead of me. Everybody laughed, and Olive's partner danced with me. But Olive was a marvellous dancer and could make any boy dance well, and of course Clayton had a wonderful time with her. Somehow he managed to get every second dance with her, and that was the end of Clayton. I know it sounds like something out of a soap opera, but that's how it happened. Clayton fell head-over-heels in love with Olive and hung around our house like a puppy. Summer holidays came and I got a job, then I went to university. Olive stayed in school until she graduated and joined the WRENs. We didn't see much of each other again after that year."

Hugh picked up a pebble from the gravel walk in front of the chair and pitched it into the trees. "So that's it."

"Yes – but the terrible thing is that Olive thinks she ruined my life. To her, being a wife and mother is everything. She thinks she deprived me of all that. Of course that's ridiculous. I realized I couldn't have the career I wanted and a family, too. I chose the career."

Hugh twisted his foot in the gravel. "Have you ever. . . ?"

"Had any affairs? None of your damned business. But I'm no virgin. I can tell you that."

"And Olive?"

"Oh, I have this little score to settle with her. She shouldn't go through life without knowing how it feels."

Chapter Five

Tom poured himself another Scotch from the little corner bar. "One thing about this reunion deal," he said. "Sure makes a man thirsty."

It was the next afternoon, and four of the Windmars were back in the living room, Shawn having gone to look up an old friend.

"Seems to me you're always thirsty," Olive scoffed. Not unkindly, not nagging, just friendly.

"Well, I'll tell you, sister dear," Tom said, standing in front of her and patting his stomach, "it's the stuff keeps me young. Sixty-seven years old and I could start raising another family."

"You'd have to get a new wife," Gwendolyn said. "I'm sure Marion has all the children and grandchildren she can handle."

"Her? Don't kid yourself. That gal's as strong as when I married her, and just as eager. I tell you – "

"Please don't bother, brother," Hugh interrupted. "We can get along without your sexual boasting."

"Sure, sure, I know," his older brother said. "But we come from hardy stock. Look at the old man – eighty-eight years old and still has more spunk than some guys half his age."

"It really is amazing how they've survived everything," Hugh mused. "You know, all the time I was growing up I never thought much of their lives."

"Yes," Olive agreed. "Dad was never one to talk much about himself."

"Would you really like to hear the story?" Gwen asked.

"Enough to sit for a few hours and listen to a tape?"

"A tape of his life? Where did you get that?"

"I made it last winter when I visited them in Florida. I taped both Mother and Dad."

"I'd sure like to hear that," Tom said. "Long as the booze holds out."

"All right, I'll play it. But I warn you, you're in for some surprises. They often have quite different versions of the same happenings. And both were remarkably frank about their lives."

William Henry's Tape

"I'm eighty-eight years old now and during my lifetime I've seen the world change more than it did in all the years up to then. I read that in the *Miami Herald* the other day. And when you think of it, well, it's true enough. The house where I was born, near Godston in old Ontario, had none of the things we have in our houses today. No electricity nor any of the things that're run by electricity. No telephone, radio, television, nothing like that. Newspapers, though. Three of them in Godston then. And magazines. We got the *Toronto Saturday Night* once a week."

"Tell me about the house where you were born."

"Made of brick. That yellow, homemade brick. House is still standing on its stone foundation. Course it's had more'n one new roof and stuff like that. But it's still there. Some bird from Toronto bought it and dammed up the stream to make a pond. Martha and I visited it a few years ago. Flew to Toronto. Five hours it took us. When we went west by train in the spring of 1912 it took us four days and three nights.

"My grandfather built that house, most of it with his own hands, after he'd got settled and had a few good years. Old log house they first lived in is still on the place. Used as a tool-shed now. This Toronto feller fixed it up, too. Hilly land. Up on the Niagara Escarpment, you understand. The Protestants settled in the hills, and the Dogans, that's the Catholics, settled on the plains below. They had the best growing land but ours was the prettiest. We had a nice little orchard, I remember, 'specially the russet apples. Man, but I did love those little hard russet-coloured rascals. Haven't seen one in years. Big tree grew right beside the barn. And bees. Father always kept bees for the honey. And we had cows, and of course horses. No tractors nor anything like that. Windmill. Two hundred acres he had. A hundred of it under cultivation. Good bottom land along the creek.

"Mostly trees on the hills, oaks and maples and beech. God, I loved those woods. Thing I missed the most when we went west was those woods. So dark and quiet. People always talk about the forest being full of birds and animals. But you never see them. The woods are silent. Silence like you never hear today."

"Were you born in the brick house?"

"Oh, yeah. We all were. All ten of us – five boys and five girls. I was the second youngest. That's why I had to leave. No living for me on that farm. Harold, the oldest boy, got it. Died there."

"Tell me about growing up on the farm."

"Work. Everybody worked. From the time you were able to walk there was something for you to do. My mother ruled the roost."

"She did?"

"Oh, yes. I tell you, Gwen, you hear a lot today about women's lib and all that, and people get the idea that women used to be meek and mild. Ain't so, believe you me. They were the strong ones. My mother, my aunts. One of my aunts was a holy terror. Wouldn't let her girls have anything to do with men. All became old maids. Yeah, the women were strong and right. Methodist right. They had God and Virtue and Right on their side and they knew it. And she could sing like an angel, my mother."

"Tell me more about her."

"Well, she wasn't Irish like my dad. She was Scotch. Poor Scotch. Family came to Canada about the same time Dad's did. They were Methodists same as Dad. Strict Methodists. I remember her, all right. Not very big, but strong. Worked from morning till night, cooking, preserving, cleaning, making butter, baking bread every second day. Never got anything out of a can. Sealers, yes. She'd put up hundreds of sealers of fruit in season. Sewing - made most of the girls' dresses. Just as your mother did when you were small."

"Yes, I remember. What did she look like, your mother?"

"Stylish. Even around the house and yard, working her head off, she always managed to look good. When she dressed up on Sunday she really was a knockout. Jet-black hair. Strong face. You've seen her picture. And full of fun, too. But strict."

"That's quite a contradiction."

"Isn't everybody full of contradictions? We say a person is good or bad, but all of us have some good and some bad in us. We say a person is serious and morose, but that same person can do a lot of laughing. And who is completely honest? There's larceny in the best of us. Not just crooked politicians and the like, but everybody. So the best I can say about my mother was that she was a human being. Fair sometimes, unfair at others. Kind most of the time but she could be unkind, too. Like the time I got all ready to go to the dance."

"What happened?"

"Well, it was a Hallowe'en dance in town, or a harvest dance. I know my older brothers worked like beavers decorating the hall with sheaves and pumpkins big as wash-tubs and bunches of apples and carrots and such. And autumn leaves. I remember those maple leaves in the fall. Beautiful. Well, the Orange Hall was a sight, I can tell you. And we all got spruced up. My first dance. I'd saved two dollars and got new shoes. And then on the very afternoon of the dance - gosh, I still can't figure it."

"What happened?"

"She said I couldn't go. No reason given. Something about being too young. See what I mean? Terrible unfair. Terrible. I'm sorry, but it still hurts to think about it.

"You see, there was a girl I was sweet on. Later on she married another guy. Often wonder what would have happened if I'd gone to that dance. Her family was Presbyterian. Hard to believe, but the Methodists hated the Presbyterians almost as much as they did the Catholics. One of the reasons I quit the church. All that hatred."

"What about your father?"

"A quiet man. Tall like me. Seem to remember him as about twice the height of my mother, but of course that's impossible. Typical Victorian. Hard-working, religious, set in his ways, bigoted; an ardent Orangeman."

"What else?"

"Nothing much."

"You are negating your own theory. You just said that there are contradictions in every person. You've told me half of what he was like. What about the other half? Was he kind, loving, considerate?"

"Yeah, he was. Never thought of it much, but now that I do think of it, he was. Like the time with the bull. We had this prime shorthorn bull, Hercules. Dad's pride and joy, cost more than all his cows put together. A shorthorn, in case you don't know, is an all-purpose breed of cattle. Good for milking, but not as good as a Holstein, and good for meat, though not as good as a Hereford or Angus. We raised them, milked them, and ate them. And shorthorn bulls are the meanest of all bulls. You got to watch them every minute. Man, but they are mean.

"Anyway, I was about ten at the time and I had strict orders about Hercules. Never go near his head and always be danged sure the door of his stall was shut and locked. Well, one day I didn't and the bull got out and into the oat bin and ate his fill of oats. Foundered himself. Died.

"Well sir, my father wasn't a swearing man. Strongest expletive he ever used was 'Oh pshaw.' But this day he ripped out a string of curses would do justice to a stevedore. I thought maybe he would kill me. I started to bawl. And you know when he saw that he just bent over and put his arms around me. First time I remember him ever touching me. He picked me up – he was a strong man – and he held me and I could see that he was crying, too. Funny, I'd forgotten that. You're making me remember things I never knew I knew."

"Yes, an interview can do that. Brings things out of the unconscious mind, that great storehouse of everything we ever did or thought. Hypnotism can do it, too."

"Isn't that a corker."

Gwendolyn stopped the tape at this point and the two sons and two daughters sat in silence. Then Gwen said, "Father was crying at this point. I'd never seen him cry before. It was a strange experience. Just as he never really knew his parents, we don't know ours."

"Turn her on again," Tom said quietly. "I'd like to know more."

The tape continued:

"You asked about school. Usual thing. Little brick one-room affair down at the corner of the Third Line and Beavis Road. About a mile from our place. Eight grades. And when we passed out of that school, got our entrance, as it was called, schooling was over for most of us. Went to work on the farm. There were twenty-two kids in that school, ranging from six to sixteen, and every last one of them was related to me. Brothers or sisters or cousins or second cousins. Families stayed close together in those days."

"What about sex education?"

"What?"

"Sex education. An important subject in school these

days, and the cause of a great deal of controversy, too. How did you learn the facts of life?"

"Facts of life, eh? Well, I'll tell you: when you live on a farm the facts of life are all around you. The cats and the dogs and the chickens and the bulls and the pigs and the horses. Seems as though something was breeding all the time. We weren't supposed to watch the stallion at work, but the snorting post was just behind the barn, under the hayloft door."

"The what post?"

"Well, you don't know everything about the facts of life, I see. The snorting post is really a pole between two posts about four feet high or so. You bring the mare up to one side of it and the stud up to the other. If she ain't ready to receive the stud she'll kick. Instead of hitting the stud in a vital spot and maybe ruining him, she hits this pole. If she don't kick, she's ready. Something like a woman saying she's got a headache."

"And as a boy you watched these - uh - proceedings from the hayloft?"

"Damn betcha. We had a ringside seat. I tell you, take a girl up there with you and it was even more fun."

"Dad!"

The tape was stopped then because the audience was convulsed with laughter.

"So the great objective psychiatrist couldn't take it," Olive laughed.

"Well, it did come as a surprise. But it made me realize something. We think sexual enlightenment is something new in the past fifty years or so, but really - "

"Been going on a long time, sister," Tom said. "Ever since Eve bit into that apple."

"Funny," Hugh mused, "but every generation has a tendency to think it invented sex. All this groping and panting and licking we see in the movies and on television amounts to nothing, really. We haven't become more open about sex, just more exhibitionist."

"And judging from the paintings and statues in galleries and museums, there's nothing new about that, either," Olive added.

"But just the same, I was surprised about Dad."

"Remember what he said on the tape there," Tom said. "Life is full of surprises."

"Points up another thing," Hugh said to Gwen. "You scientists are everlastingly carrying on studies, often at considerable public expense, to prove something people have always known. Such as getting a half-million-dollar grant to prove that tall people can reach higher than short people."

"Your short reach would tend to prove that," his sister replied icily.

"Oh-oh, here we go again," Olive said. "Right back to where we used to be."

"Yeah," Tom agreed. "Better start rolling that tape so we can all pick on the old man."

"Why did you go out west?"

"Well, to tell you the truth, there wasn't room for me in Ontario – all the good land was already taken. In the west, good land was free for anybody who'd work for it. First went west in 1910, when I was eighteen years old. Harvest time. What they called a 'harvest special.' Western farmers were raising good crops but they needed help to stook and thresh them. I saw this ad in a paper, put in by the CPR. 'Forty thousand farm labourers needed in the west. Twelve dollars to Winnipeg.' So I went.

"It was something of an adventure, don't you see. And the first time I saw the prairies – all that land just covered with ripening grain – well, I tell you I couldn't believe it. Miles and miles and miles – as far as you could see in every direction. The bread-basket of the world, they called it, and it surely was.

"Right then and there I fell in love with the prairies. Every town we came to along the track there were farmers standing on the wooden platforms waiting to hire hands. Sometimes they'd come to the train window or get on and offer us jobs. So I got off with some other fellows I'd made friends with on the way out and hired on with a man named McIntosh. This was in southern Manitoba, which was pretty well settled. He had a big spread, two sections I think, that's twelve hundred and eighty acres. Big house painted white, made of lumber. All the houses I'd known had been brick.

"Well sir, I tell you that was some threshing outfit. Big steam engine puffing away, burning straw. Eight bundle teams. They're the ones that haul the racks full of wheat sheaves to the separator. Grain haulers. Straw boy, whose job it was to haul straw to the engine from the straw stack. Field pitcher, spikers, separator man, foreman. A big threshing gang. Ah, it was wonderful.

"But hard work. Up at four. Dark as pitch. Into the big barn with lanterns. Harness your team. Then into the cookhouse for breakfast. Meat and potatoes and eggs and pie and cake. Much as you could stuff in. You'd need it. Out to the field at the first light and start loading up your rack with sheaves. Man, that's hard work, but being from the farm I was used to it. But some of the city fellers, it almost killed them. One guy had blisters on his hands big as golf balls, I'll swear. Lunch in the field about ten o'clock, brought out by the boss's daughter. Dinner at twelve and then work till sundown. Then a big supper and fall into bed until four the next morning. Seven days a week as long as the weather held. I'd have stayed on there if it hadn't been for the accident."

"Accident?"

"Yeah, it was a bloody mess. Never been able to get it out of my mind. Made me a lot more careful around a feeder, I can tell you."

"What happened?"

"City kid, name of Jimmy Smithers. From Winnipeg, out there to make some money for his fall high-school term. Not very big, but funny. Lord, he was a funny kid. Full of jokes. And limericks. 'A mathematician named

Hall had a rectangular ball.' He had a million of them. A regular comedian that boy was. And he could recite poetry, Keats and Shelley and Shakespeare. Often wonder what would have become of that boy."

"Tell me about the accident."

"Well, the feeder is the thing sticks out in front of the separator at the top. About five feet long and maybe three wide. It's got a revolving belt on it, made out of canvas. You throw a sheaf onto the belt and it moves into the knives that are whirling around to cut the twine off the sheaves. Then the sheaf goes through a big drum called a cylinder; that chews it up and starts the process of separating the grain kernels from the chaff and straw. That's why they call it a separator. The separator was about twenty-five feet long - you can see them in agricultural museums - with the feeder at one end and the blower at the other. The straw went out the blower and the wheat went into a hopper and down a spout to a grain box to be hauled to the grain elevator in town.

"Well, when you had a load of sheaves, or bundles, about ten or fifteen feet high, you had to drive your team up beside that separator with all its pulleys and belts whirling and rattling away. As close as you could get, see? And you had to stand up on the load so you could see where you were going. It was scary the first time and Jimmy was always nervous about it. Well, about the third day - it was a beautiful day - Jimmy was first in to the machine. He picked up that first big sheaf on the end of his fork and was going to pitch it into the feeder. I don't know how it happened, but the tine of the fork caught on the twine around the sheaf and wouldn't let go. Now one of those sheaves weighs up to thirty pounds. He should have let go the fork and let it go through the knives. Would have made a mess. But he didn't. Held on and quick as a wink he and the bundle and the fork all landed on the feeder. Separator man saw it and yelled at the engine man, but it was too late. Poor

Jimmy was pulled right into those knives.

"God, I'll never forget it, pulling him out of there. Blood all over the place, a hundred cuts. He lived a little while, but soon bled to death. Just before he died he looked at me and muttered something that sounded like, 'I always was a cut-up.' "

"That's terrible."

"Yeah. Farms are dangerous places. I've had my share of accidents, like the time I lost this finger. Well, anyway, that shut the outfit down for a couple of days. I drew my pay, two dollars a day, and moved on. Just as easily could have been me that fell into that feeder. I figured that outfit was bad luck. Poor Jimmy.

"I caught a train in town and went farther west. Got off near Regina and hired on with another outfit. Worked there until it was time to go home. But I didn't want to go. All the talk was about the free land they were giving out in the Edenvale district. Homesteads. So before I left I went to the land office in Regina and got all the information about getting a homestead."

"Why didn't you just stay then?"

"If I had I'd never have met your mother, and what a shame that would have been. No, I was sure I wanted to move west, but I needed some money for buildings and equipment. So as soon as I got home I went into Godston and got a job in a bank. A junior. Spent most of my time peddling drafts to the Godston businessmen. I was a regular Peter Pupkin. Got into the drama club and played tennis and skated and had a great time. Sure was different from the farm. No women working in banks then. All men. Now, except for the manager, you don't see any men. Women are taking over the world."

"Father!"

"They are, Gwennie. Oh, I don't mean that in any male-chauvinist-pig way. It's just a fact. And a good thing, too, I say when you look at the mess men have made of the world. England's got a woman prime minister. So has India. Israel had one. It's coming. You see, women are smarter than men. Look at your school days. The girls were always at the top of the class. Look at you, the only Ph.D. in the family. Hughie might have made it if it hadn't been for the Depression; we couldn't support him in university. Hughie is smart. Bitter, but smart."

"Why is he bitter, Father?"

"Lots of reasons. You may find out some day. Where was I? How in hell did I get on to this talk about women? Oh, yes, the bank. I had a great time as a young banker. We used to have tobogganing parties in those days out in the hills. Man, but they were fun. Finish up with a bonfire, roast some wieners, and have tea. Sit out there in the crisp air and sing songs. 'There's a long, long trail a-winding.' There sure is, kid. Like everybody that age, we thought we would never grow old. But we did.

"Well, anyway, the bank moved me to Toronto. Carlton Street branch. Across the street from where Maple Leaf Gardens is now. Let's see, that would be in 1911. I was nineteen years old then. Oh, I tell you, Toronto was a grand place then. Theatres, ferry rides, skating in the old Mutual Street arena, dances. And, best of all, I met your mother."

"How did it come about, this perfect marriage?"

"Perfect marriage? There ain't no such thing. Some might seem like it, but that's because they've done a good job of compromising. Compromise, that's the name of the game in marriage. Natural, because women and men are different. Different in the way they feel, their hormones, different in the things that are important to them, different in their urges and drives. So it's compromise from the word go.

"Starts right off at the wedding. Most men want it simple. Elope, get it over with. A big wedding is just an impediment to jumping into bed together. But to a woman a big wedding is something she's been dreaming about since she was a little girl, and her mother's been dreaming about it, too. So right off they have to compromise on that. And it never ends. Martha and I are still compromising. Couples who can't compromise break up. Simple as that."

"Hmm. You were going to tell me how you met."

"Chance. An accident. Boy meets girl. You know, we scoff at the boy-meets-girl plots out of Hollywood, but a lot of true stories make those plots look sick. That's the way it works, and a good thing. Now you take if I'd stayed in Godston near my own family; in due course I'd have married a woman from a farm down the road and that would have been that. Soon as I left the farm I set in motion a whole new set of chance happenings. And then to Toronto. Never could have met a girl like your mother out there in Godston.

"Anyhow, about meeting Martha. We used to go down to the Mutual Street arena, a few blocks south of where I boarded, to skate. Everybody skated there. Still do, I understand. They had music, great skating music. Skating was like dancing. You took a girl skating and you skated to music and you romanced her. Couples who couldn't skate together weren't likely to get together.

"Funny thing – I wasn't going to go to the rink that night because the girl I was going with got the sniffles. If she hadn't there's a good chance she would have been your ma. Anyway, my roommate Harry Binns, a great guy – he was later killed at Vimy Ridge – he talked me into going with him.

"Well, I was quite a skater in those days and so was Harry. We both played on the bank hockey team. We were showing off. While the others skated around in a big circle we were doing our stunts in the middle, all sorts of fancy turns and leaps and all that stuff. Showing off."

"And you ran into her."

"No, nothing like that. She was there with another fellow who wasn't a very good skater, just average, and she'd been watching us strut our stuff out there. So when the music stopped, by ding if she didn't skate up to me where I was standing leaning against the boards and ask me to skate with her.

"Well, you could have knocked me over with a feather. Girls just didn't do that. But, you see, that's the thing: Martha was no ordinary girl. She was full of adventure and daring, with more gumption than ten girls. And believe me, she needed it when we moved out to the homestead. Soon as I took her hand the whole world changed for me. How do you explain it? I'd known lots of other girls. Some prettier than Martha, some sweet, some full of fun, but right there and then something happened that had never happened to me before. You call it what you like. You're the psychologist. Probably got an explanation having something to do with electricity or such. I just call it love at first sight."

"Yes, I know the feeling."

"You do? You? What happened?"

"You never knew, did you? Right under your nose and you never saw. Well, that's another story. Tell me, Father, what was Mother like then?"

"What was she like? Can't tell you what she looked like, only what she looked like to me. We don't see people with our eyes, you know, but with our minds, or hearts, or whatever you want to call it. Well, she was small, still is, lovely blue eyes and she still has. Her hair? She's worn it so many different ways over the years that I'd have to look at an old picture to remember how it was then. But mostly she was a toucher."

"A toucher?"

"Liked to touch people. Lay her hand on your arm when she was talking to you. Take your hand when she was walking with you. Just touch a lot."

"Recent experiments have proved that touching is an important adjunct to well-being. People who touch are healthier, recover from heart attacks faster, even if they are only touching pets."

"It took experiments to find that out? Shucks, I could have told them that and saved a lot of money."

"Yes, I'm sure you could have. But not everybody realizes the value of touching. That's why we must have proof. It often seems, I know, that a lot of sociological experiments just prove the obvious, but, don't forget, the obvious is often what people refuse to believe.

"And so you were married. Tell me how that came about."

"Well, I suppose if this account is to be worth anything it should tell the truth, as they say, the whole truth and nothing but the truth. Can't do anybody any harm now. Fact is, the date of our wedding, the wedding anniversary we've been celebrating all these years, the one we're celebrating this year, isn't exactly accurate. We moved it back a couple of months so's Tom could have the regulation nine months' time, if you see what I mean. Martha was almost two months' pregnant when we got married. Can you imagine taking a pregnant girl out to a lonely prairie homestead? I can't when I think of it now, but then I'm a few years older than I was then. Anyway, it came close to killing us both."

When the tape stopped, nobody said anything for a few seconds, then Hugh burst out.

"Well, I'm damned! So you were a love child, Tom!"

"The very best kind," Tom said. "Always knew I was special."

Hugh was thoughtful. "I dare say that story was repeated hundreds of times by restless people from Ontario. Restless and not afraid to take a chance."

"How did you ever get Dad to open up like that?" Olive marvelled. "He was always such a quiet man. You know, never said anything, hardly."

Hugh laughed. "I suspect the reason we thought Dad was quiet was because the rest of us were so noisy. Always talking, laughing, shouting, arguing. The poor guy never got a chance to open his mouth."

"That's for damned sure," Tom agreed. "We were some noisy bunch. But I used to hear him talking to Ma after they went to bed. He'd tell her all about what happened during the day, 'specially when he was in the construction business. Still does, I bet."

"Yes," Olive agreed. "In bed's about the only time people with kids get to talk to each other."

"I'd sure like to know more of this," Tom said. "Got anything on Ma, Gwennie?"

"Yes, as a matter of fact I have. Plenty. Would you like to hear it?"

"I would," Hugh said. "Learning about the folks might give this reunion some purpose."

"Oh you," Olive snapped. "You make me sick, you really do."

Gwen pressed on. "I talked to Mother for hours. Some on tape and some I'll just have to remember. If you like I'll tell you what she said when she's out at her library board meeting."

Chapter Six

Gwen's story was interrupted by the arrival of their mother.

"My goodness, but it's nice to see you all sitting here together," Martha said as she entered the room. Shawn returned with her, and the family was back together again.

Tom leaped to his feet and took his mother's arm.

"Here, Ma, you sit over here in the place of honour. Hugh, get your ass out of Ma's chair."

"Tom!" Gwen admonished.

Martha's face lit up with a smile. Most of her wrinkles disappeared and her eyes sparkled.

"Don't worry, Gwen dear, I'm used to Tom's language. Like his father, he never uses a long word when a four-letter one will do. At my age, I don't let things like that bother me."

"Nonsense, Mother," Gwen said. "Age has nothing to do with it."

"Thank you, dear. Do you know, Albert, my hairdresser, said I didn't look a day over seventy. Imagine that."

"Hairdressers always say that to elderly ladies," Shawn said. "Improves the tip."

His mother looked sad for a moment. Shawn never did have any tact.

"Don't listen to Shawn, Ma," Hugh said. "He's just a kid."

"Oh, God. How old do you have to be in this family before they stop saying you're just a kid? I'm forty-six years old, for gosh sake!"

"Forty-six!" Gwen said. "It doesn't seem possible. That

means you were only ten years old when the war ended. Do you remember anything about it?"

"I just barely remember when the war started, and Alvin said – " He stopped.

But Martha was thinking of something else. "Gracious, I almost forgot. I must go and meet Dorothy for that library board meeting." She got up and left the room.

"Doesn't Mother look well for her age?" Olive said proudly.

"She most certainly does," Gwen said. "But she comes by it naturally. One of our ancestors, a great-great-grandmother I think it was, lived to be a hundred and four."

"How about that?" Tom said. "Ma'll probably top that, the way she's going. And she's had a hard life, too."

"Indeed she has," Gwen agreed.

"Okay, Gwen," Tom said. "How's about telling us all you learned about Ma."

"Well, you all know some of this, so you'll just have to forgive me if I sometimes state the obvious." She smiled ruefully. "Hugh would say that's a characteristic of people with Ph.D.s."

"Touché," Hugh said. "What has always impressed me about Mother is, well, for lack of a better word, her class."

"She always was a classy woman, that's for sure," Tom agreed.

"Well," Gwen went on, "she knew how to wear clothes, and how to make them. Remember she came from a wealthy family in the most fashionable part of Toronto. And for a while she went to one of the best girls' schools in the city."

"But how did she handle those terrible days on the homestead?" Olive asked. "You'd think that would take the spirit out of anyone."

"That's what I wanted to find out, and I think I did. She was strong and healthy and extremely high-spirited with a great sense of humour and great fortitude. We can all consider ourselves lucky for having such a parent. Both parents, really."

"What got me," Hugh said, "was how she kept up with

everything that was going on even though she was shut off from newspapers. And of course there was no radio. I never could quite understand that."

"Well," Gwen explained, "her older sister, Mary, who lived in Toronto, sent her subscriptions to *Mayfair* and *The New Yorker*, so that Mother always knew what was going on in Toronto and New York, what plays were on Broadway and what Woolcott Gibbs thought of them. When *Anything Goes* became a hit she learned the song 'The Best Things in Life Are Free' and taught it to us.

"She was on the library board, making sure that the best of the world's literature was available to all, especially to her. She read philosophy, fiction, travel, and medicine. She kept herself informed.

"In the mid-twenties, when she and Father were able to afford a radio, her contact with Toronto and New York and other parts of the world became more intimate. When finally they were able to visit those places, and London and Paris and Rome, it was like visiting well-remembered and much-loved scenes.

"Mother was born in a large brick house with turrets in the Rosedale district of Toronto. Her father, Doctor Timothy O'Neil, was a mainstay of the famous Hospital for Sick Children; her mother, Susan, had always worked as a volunteer in the same institution. Which may have been one of the reasons Mother survived the epidemics of gastroenteritis, which every August carried off dozens of babies in Toronto.

"Her father had often described to Mother how, in the middle of the night, he lashed his fine driving horse through the curving streets of Rosedale and down Yonge Street to the corner of Yonge and College and then west to the hospital. But he always said that rather than any treatment it was her own strong constitution that enabled her to survive the vomiting and diarrhoea that so dehydrated the tiny bodies and killed them.

"Mother's was a happy childhood. Her father was rich and famous in the city; her mother was energetic and beautiful, and introduced her to the beautiful things and saw to it that she was protected from the ugly. Her sister, who was two years older, was fun to tag after and taught her how to do her hair in the most attractive ways. Mother went to the Methodist Church Sunday school and joined the Mission Band and the Temperance League. At an early age she took the pledge never to sully her beautiful body with the demon rum. She attended dancing classes and took elocution lessons and as soon as she was old enough enrolled in the fashionable Havergal College, on Jarvis Street just north of Carlton.

"Her life was all planned for her. She would go to the University of Toronto after Havergal, and there she would meet a promising young doctor or lawyer or future premier of the province and they would be married and in all probability live in Rosedale, where they would raise two or possibly three children.

"This was her mother's plan for her. But Mother never thought much about it. She was too interested in plays and concerts and romantic literature, and most especially in boys.

"Even as a small child she was a flirt, she told me."

"All little girls are flirts, and most big ones, too," Tom said.

"Yes," Gwen agreed, "but some, like Mother, have a talent for it that supersedes natural coquetry. She was a toucher and a climber on knees, especially male knees. And when, as often happened, her boy cousins came to visit, she usually managed to get one of them off into the ravine behind the house for special games. Kissing games were her favourite. She'd seen lots of pictures of kissing, and seen it on the stage. Her games never went past kissing and patting, but she felt an excitement that was hard to control. She wasn't a bad girl or, as the saying went then, a 'bold girl,' rather an affectionate, loving girl, very sexy.

"It worried her parents, who spotted it early. 'She's vulnerable,' she heard Grandpa say. 'Terribly vulnerable. If she comes into contact with the wrong person she could be ruined. It's our job to see to it that she doesn't.' Being a doctor, he was better able than most to give her what were usually referred to as 'the facts of life.' They consisted mostly of warnings against venereal disease, of which he'd seen plenty, and pregnancy, of which he'd seen even more.

"Mother's mother hinted broadly that 'nice girls didn't,' and stressed the value of a good reputation. 'Once a girl loses her reputation, she is finished.'

"All of which, of course, did little to curb Mother's high spirits and adventuresome nature. She felt that the plan mapped out for her by her parents was mundane and dull. She dreamed of running off to New York to become a glamorous actress.

"She grew tired of Havergal. 'Too stuffy,' she said. She envied the girls who went to Jarvis Collegiate, almost right across the street. They had so much more freedom and so much more fun. Besides, there were boys at Jarvis. Lots of boys, football players and hockey players, and it was to these that she was drawn. And so, despite her parents' protests, she quit Havergal and enrolled at Jarvis.

" 'A group of us used to go to all the games,' she told me. 'We weren't cheer-leaders, but we sure cheered. Called ourselves "the Daffy Dozen" and we always sat together or stood together at the football games and made up songs about the players and cheered our heads off. The boys gave us plenty to cheer about, too. Seems to me they always beat other teams, Parkdale and Harbord. I guess I fell in and out of love a dozen times at Jarvis Collegiate.'

"She went tobogganing in High Park and skating on Grenadier Pond, which was reputed to have no bottom. And she skated to music at Mutual Street arena.

" 'It was a great time to be young in Toronto,' Mother said, 'especially if you were rich and high-spirited and healthy.'

"At the age of seventeen she graduated from Jarvis Collegiate. She had already had three proposals, not exactly proposals of marriage, but proposals to become engaged. Being engaged was fun and she would do it for a while and then return the boy's ring when she spotted a more desirable beau.

"Her father was worried by her fickleness but her mother knew better. 'Just you wait, Timothy,' she would say. 'One of these days this girl will really fall in love, and when she does it will be forever.'

"Her mother knew, of course, because she had been that way herself. 'I just hope you will be as lucky as I was,' she used to say to Mother.

"But Timothy was still sceptical. His orderly, disciplined mind could never understand his daughter, but then he had never fully understood his wife, either. Never understood that chance had played him a good trick when it brought him into contact with her. He always attributed it to his own good judgement and the thing he valued above all else, common sense.

"Mother's older sister, Mary, was more like her father. She followed the pattern. At the age of nineteen, she married a lawyer ten years her senior who was just beginning a career that would lead him into provincial and then federal politics.

"She had a big wedding in the Timothy Eaton Memorial Church, with the pews filled with Toronto's finest, and then a reception at the Granite Club with hundreds of guests and the carriages lined up for blocks along St. Clair Avenue.

"Mother was a bridesmaid and she loved it, although she disgraced herself by giggling when the Reverend McLeod said 'Love, honour, and obey.' She thought she would like to have just such a wedding herself some day, but somehow doubted that she ever would.

"In the meantime she was having too much fun to worry about it. She was waiting for someone who would give her goose-bumps. 'I didn't exactly know what goose-bumps were. Probably picked up the term from one of the romantic novels I was always reading,' she said.

"And for some reason she was sure she was more likely to meet 'Mr. Right,' a term in common use then, in the business world than at university. And so it was that she surprised her father one day in the fall of 1910 by informing him that she had enrolled in the business college, which was upstairs in a house on the corner of Yonge and College streets, and that she would require from him one hundred and fifty dollars for tuition.

" 'Why in the name of all that's holy do you think you want to go to business college? That's for working girls.'

" 'I intend to be a working girl.'

" 'But dear,' her mother admonished, 'working long hours in a stuffy office, especially in the summer! You've never really spent a summer in the city.'

" 'Fiddle-faddle. I can stand it if other girls can.'

" 'Other girls are more used to it. You've never worked, dear. You don't know what it's like.'

" 'Then it's time I learned.'

"Her parents gave in, of course, because there was nothing else they could do.

"Mother laughed about this part. Dressed in a sensible middy and skirt, she climbed the two flights of stairs to Webster Perkins' Business College. On the first day Perkins gave a little speech to the fourteen boys and five girls in attendance, saying that his school had high standards and they would have to work hard. 'Pitman shorthand,' he said, 'may be a short way of writing, but it takes a good deal of learning. Along with typing and bookkeeping, there is much to learn by spring and any girls or young men who think they are here for a good time had better think again.' He was right. One of the girls in the class was Elsie Goodman, who lived on a farm fifty miles north of Toronto. She'd been to high school in a small town and had never been in the city before. But, like Mother, she was a lively girl with a mind of her own. She loved skating and dancing and plays and especially boys. 'We were like two peas in a pod,' Mother told me. Elsie roomed at the YWCA, a short distance away on McGill Street, and, because money was scarce, she needed a roommate. Mother decided to move in with her.

" 'I'm just asking you to lend me the money,' she told

her father. 'I'll pay it back when I get my first job.'

" 'It's not the money, dear,' her mother said. 'But really, living downtown unsupervised.'

" 'Unsupervised my foot! You should see the rules and regulations they have at that place. They're far stricter than you are!'

"They proved to be too strict for Mother and Elsie, and it wasn't long before they moved out of the YWCA and into a rooming house on Church Street, across from the Model School, where young men and women were taught to be teachers.

"But, more important, it was close to a bank on the corner of College and Church, where Mother did her banking.

" 'When I walked into that bank I was a goner,' Mother said to me. She didn't know exactly what it was that attracted her about the tall lean man who seemed uncomfortable in his store suit. She only knew she was attracted. Trouble was, he didn't pay any attention to her at all. Since he hadn't reached teller status, Father didn't deal with customers; he was always at a desk or walking from one desk to another in the murky interior of the bank, beyond the tellers' cage.

" 'He didn't know I existed,' she said, 'and it made me that mad, because I was busting to meet him. And then one evening at the rink I saw my chance and, by cracky, I took it.' "

Chapter Seven

"Hey, don't stop now," Tom said. "You're just getting to the really good stuff."

Gwen went on with her story. "In the fall of 1911 Mother was eighteen years old, attractive, lively, intelligent, and adventuresome, and terribly determined to live her life the way she wanted to live it.

"Although Toronto was an exciting place to live for a young woman who was on her own and had a good job, it was not what Mother wanted. What did she want? She really didn't know. She only knew that she was restless and eager and that something very important was lacking in her life.

"When she met William Henry Windmar at the Mutual Street arena and skated with him, she knew she had found what she wanted. And when she learned that Dad was determined to go west, she was even more sure of it.

"Going west was the exciting thing to do in those years. It represented change and adventure and independence. It appealed to the wanderlust and restlessness in many an Ontarian, descendants of wanderers who had never been content to remain in England or Scotland or Ireland but had ventured into new lands and new experiences.

"On Mother's first date with Father, he took her to dinner at the King Edward Hotel and then to the Royal Alexandra Theatre to see 'The Only Way.' Mother wept quietly at the noble sacrifice of Sidney Carton. She knew it wasn't quite proper for a girl to go on dates with young men unchaperoned, but Will was different. Besides, she couldn't keep her eyes and hands off him.

"When he took her home they stood at the door of her room and she wondered if he was going to kiss her. She wanted him to so badly that she could hardly stand it. He thanked her for the date and started to leave.

" 'Won't you come in?' she said.

" 'Well, gosh, thanks.'

" 'I'll make you some tea and I think there is a piece of cake left.'

" 'Cake? I'm pretty full after what we had.'

" 'Oh, Will, don't be a fuddy-dud.' She grabbed him by the arm and pulled him into the room. It was a large front room with three alcove windows, tastefully furnished with a couch at one side that made into two beds and a make-shift kitchen at the other. In the centre were a small table and some easy chairs. The walls were covered with paintings.

"Mother said she could tell that Will had never been in a girl's room before.

" 'Gosh, this is nice,' he said.

" 'Thank you,' Mother said. 'Sit in that chair there. It's the most comfortable.' She remembers every word of that conversation.

" 'Uh, where's your roommate?' Father asked.

" 'She went home for the weekend.'

" 'Gosh!'

" 'Not so loud, please. I don't think Mrs. Black approves of her roomers entertaining young men in their rooms, although I've never tried. You are my very first.'

" 'Well, I'm honoured.'

"What was it, Mother often wondered afterwards, that made him so attractive to her, that made everything he said so fascinating, that made the way he rubbed his face when he was thinking so devastating? And that mouth of his. How could she get him to kiss her?

"It was a completely new experience for her. She had flirted with men, often, but it was always just fun. This was different. She felt hot all over and her heart was pounding.

" 'Isn't it awfully hot in here?' she asked.

" 'Well, kind of.'

" 'Would you like to take off your jacket?'

" 'Yeah, sure.' He took off his jacket. 'Would you mind if I take off this blasted collar, too? It's been choking me to death all evening.'

"Will was wearing a stiff wing collar, the fashion then, and being a farm boy he had never got used to it, even though he was required to wear it in the bank all day.

" 'Of course,' she said. 'By all means take off your collar – and your vest, too.'

"It was all perfectly innocent, of course, and quite silly. Then it became a game. But I suppose most sex is a game. As often happens when two people are in love, the game takes them to the point of no return.

"Mother could no more have stopped the game than she could have stopped breathing. And she didn't want to. She'd always known this would happen to her some time and she had always hoped it would be with the right man. Now she was sure, and so it was a natural, loving act.

"And although both were novices there was no awkwardness or fumbling or shame. Which was strange when she thought of it afterwards, considering that both had been raised in strict Methodist families.

"Mother had never read books about sex, or long-winded magazine articles about freedom and self-expression and being uninhibited by the joys of the orgasm, but that didn't matter. She simply did what came naturally and afterwards felt no shame or guilt.

"There was one big difference between then and now. She wasn't on the pill, simply because it hadn't been developed, and Father was too impulsive and spontaneous to be carrying a rubber condom in a neat little envelope. And so the natural consequence was that Mother became pregnant. Maybe that was a bad thing, maybe a good thing. No one can say for sure.

"As for her, she really wasn't worried. After that first encounter she and Father enjoyed each other many times.

And when her period failed to come she wasn't frantic. When she told Father about it, he naturally was concerned about not having as much money as he could have wished to get married, but there was never any doubt in either of their minds that they would get married.

"No one was outraged. Short-term pregnancies were common in those days. It was said that the first baby might take anywhere from seven to nine months, while subsequent ones always went the full nine months.

"Mother's solution to the problem was straightforward. 'We'll go west and live on your homestead. We'll set our wedding date to suit the circumstances and nobody in Saskatchewan will know the difference,' she said to Father.

"And so, on the twenty-fourth of April 1912, they were married in the big house in Rosedale with just the family present. Mother's mother wept a little because it was the thing to do and Grampa took Father aside and said, 'Look, you're going to need money. A big wedding would have cost me at least a thousand dollars. Here's a cheque for that amount.'

"Father took the cheque in the spirit it was offered because he needed the money, and right after the wedding he and Mother boarded the CPR Transcontinental at Union Station and started west.

"Right from the beginning they had their problems, caused not by the narrowness and meanness of people but by the meanness of Mother Nature and the fickle gods of luck. Wind and frost and blizzards and drought and grasshoppers and accidents. There were no wild Indians to bother them, but there was a wild, wild wind, far more persistent and menacing than any Indian, real or imagined.

"The train journey west was a horror for Mother. There was no sleeping car or diner; she and Father took some food with them and bought sandwiches from a concessionaire who came through the train hawking his wares. The seats were hard slats and were uncomfortable, almost impossible to sleep on. There was no air conditioning and the train was unbearably hot and stuffy.

"Worst of all, Martha was one of those unfortunate women who suffer from morning sickness. In her case it lasted most of the day, and she spent a good deal of the trip in the cramped confines of the tiny toilet at the end of the car.

"For a nineteen-year-old used to the comforts of the city, the trip was a terrible ordeal but, as she often said later, 'It was a good introduction for worse things to come.'

"Through it all, Father's enthusiasm for his chosen land never abated. When they left the spruce forests of northern Ontario and hit the prairie land of southern Manitoba, he was ecstatic, alternating between sympathy for his bride and excitement over what he was seeing from the train window.

" 'How is your tummy now, darling?' he would ask and, without waiting for an answer, he would shout, 'Look at that land! Far as you can see, flat, fertile land. We'll have land like that. Just wait and see!'

"Mother said she tried to be enthusiastic, but any mention of her tummy tended to upset it anew and she would dash for the toilet at the other end of the car.

"After what seemed an endless time they reached Winnipeg, the principal distributing and shipping centre for the three prairie provinces and already a fair-sized city. They were able to get a good meal in the station restaurant and, freed from the rocking, jolting motion of the railway car, Mother was able to keep it down. Without that meal, she believed, she would have perished from malnutrition and dehydration before they reached Regina.

" 'How far is it now?' she asked when they were back in their seats.

" 'Well, about five hundred miles to Regina, then a few more to the homestead.'

" 'How many more?'

" 'I'm not sure, exactly. It's in the western section of the province. What they call the Kindersley-Rosetown district. Very good farm land.'

"The trip from Winnipeg to Regina was dreary. Mile

after mile of flat, treeless prairie; thousands upon thousands of acres of flat land. In the ditches next to the tracks the spring runoff had collected in pools which were full of black-faced coots and blackbirds and ducks. Once, in the distance, they saw an antelope bounding across the prairie; small ground squirrels scurried in the fields, found their holes and sat up like tent pegs, flicking their tails.

" 'They call them gophers,' Father explained. 'But they aren't like the gophers in Ontario, which live entirely underground. Another name for these little rascals is flickertails. You can see why.'

"Mother was feeling better and her natural good nature and cheerfulness returned. She was delighted with everything she saw. 'Look at that man ploughing with cows!' she exclaimed.

" 'Oxen,' Father told her. He realized that she was going to a new and strange country to live on a farm, and that she knew nothing about farming. And so he set about teaching her.

" 'The first thing we have to get,' he explained, 'is a good team of horses and a wagon. A plough and a set of harrows and of course a cow, some chickens, and a few pigs. And right away, even before we plant any crops, we've got to make a good, big garden. We're lucky there're already buildings on the place.'

" 'I love gardening. May I have flowers?'

" 'Acres of them.'

" 'Oh, I wish we'd get there.'

"Thinking about it afterwards, Mother wondered how they did it. A nineteen-year-old pregnant woman who had never been on a farm was suddenly required to do all the things a farm wife must do. But they were young and full of energy and hope.

"Finally they reached Regina, the capital of Saskatchewan. Pile o' Bones had been its original name, because of the bleached buffalo bones stacked near the freight sheds awaiting shipment to the east. It was a flat town with wide, dusty streets and hastily constructed frame buildings.

"From Regina they took one of the spur lines that were spreading across Saskatchewan like capillaries from an artery: they went northwest for another hundred miles to the town of Edenvale. Like the other new towns sprouting up at ten-mile intervals along the tracks, Edenvale was a collection of shacks; the town supplied all the pioneers needed, from tea to ploughs.

"Here Father bought a team of horses and a wagon, which they loaded with the bare necessities. Then they started off along a rutted trail for their homestead, somewhere on the flat prairie roughly four miles away.

"Thus they began their new life, full of hope and doubts and with a family well on the way. Like thousands of others, they would make it or not according to luck, chance, hard work, and the vagaries of the most capricious climate on the continent." Gwen leaned back in her chair.

"So that's why they came west," Tom said when his sister had stopped. "I suppose in a way it was my fault."

"Nonsense," Hugh said. "They'd have come anyway. Dad was so hung up on the rich prairie soil."

"What I want to hear about is their life on the homestead," Shawn said with enthusiasm. "Gad, that must have been great."

"Greater to hear about than to live, I bet," Olive said.

"Well," Gwen said. "I have that part on tape. If you'll be patient I'll set it up for you."

Chapter Eight

"Tell me about the homestead, Mother." Gwen's voice came from the tape recorder.

"The homestead? Oh dear, that was so long ago I don't know how much I can recall. I do remember the prairie fire, though. Oh, my, that was terrible! You could see it coming, you know, from the west. Just a line of flames coming right towards the house and barn. There was no way to put it out or stop it, no water of course, nor hoses. Will and Harry, the man who was working with us that year, worked like darkies to plough a fireguard between us and the fire. And I loaded the children into the buggy. . . ."

"How old were they?"

"Well, there were just two then. Let me see, Tom would be four and Hughie two. And I was pregnant, of course. I always seemed to be pregnant. It's funny, you know, if we'd had the pill then, some of you would never have been born at all."

"I'm glad you didn't have the pill."

"Yes, so am I, now. But at the time - well, it was difficult. Anyway, I put the two boys in the buggy. Both the horses were pulling the plough, to make the firebreak. So I pulled the buggy myself, just as fast as I could go, away from the fire."

"What happened?"

"I don't know what would have happened if they hadn't got that firebreak ploughed. But they did, just in time. Saved the house and barn and even a stack of oat sheaves. The grass was always dry in the spring after the snow had gone. Just like tinder.

"Will was that tired when he finished. Almost dead. Covered with soot and sweat. He just collapsed into bed without eating a thing. I'll never forget that fire."

"Did you ever find out how the fire got started?"

"Oh, yes, indeed. That young scamp, Orville Ferguson. They lived two miles west of us. Seems he was playing with matches. His father warmed his britches, I can tell you."

"Tell me about getting to the homestead, Mother, everything you can remember. When did you arrive there?"

"In the spring. We set out from Edenvale with a wagon and a team of horses. And on that wagon was everything we thought we would need. A good cookstove – that was important – and a small Quebec heater. A table and two chairs. And a mattress. That's all the furniture we could take because we had to have room for the plough and the harrow, you see. And pails of flour and sugar and tea. And of course potatoes. Couldn't do without them.

"And Bessie, that was the name of the cow Will bought. You see, he'd had a cow named Bessie on the farm at home and he thought giving ours the same name was lucky. Oh, dear, that cow! The number of times I milked her. It was funny, you know, because at first I didn't know the first thing about milking a cow – or anything else around the farm, for that matter. Will milked her on the way, but when we got to the homestead I had to take over the job because there were so many other things for him to do. I soon learned, I can tell you. That and a lot of other things, like making bread and churning butter and building fires and cutting wood. . . ."

"The buildings. Tell me what you remember about them."

"Well, there was a shack on the homestead that the man who first had it had built. Thank goodness for that shack. And a shed for the cow. We were much better off than some. We had glass windows and real doors, one at the front and another at the back. And do you know that from that front door I couldn't see anything but prairie, miles and miles of prairie. Oh, there was a slough on the other side of the house and a grove of poplars and willows. They called them bluffs. And there was a well. A good well with a pump on it. Thank heaven. The water was kind of sulphurous, like a lot of water in the country, but it was clean. The well had been cribbed and had a good top, so snakes and things couldn't get into it."

"Weren't you afraid away out there alone?"

"No, there was nothing out there to hurt us. No wild Indians, as some people thought. Oh, we saw Indians once in a while, but they were a sorry-looking lot. Not very wild. Usually hungry, poor things. And Will was never far away."

"But a hundred and sixty acres is a big space."

"Oh, yes. What I really did worry about was how isolated we were from a doctor. We certainly couldn't run to a doctor every time a child got the sniffles. I guess the worst time was when Tommy got appendicitis. Oh, that was awful!"

"What did you do?"

"Well, he got this terrible pain in the abdomen, on the right side, and he was vomiting and had a high temperature. All the signs of appendicitis. We were up all night with him. Poor little tad, he cried with the pain. And it took a lot to make Tom cry. In the morning we hitched up the buggy and drove the four miles into town. Of course there was no doctor there, either. So there was nothing for it but to get on the train and take him to Regina. There were two trains a day then.

"Well, he survived, but we were always afraid of blood poisoning and meningitis and things like that. Our neighbour lost a child with that. But you know, there wasn't the same chance of children catching things as there was in Toronto. I remember Daddy saying there'd be an epidemic of polio every summer, usually the time the CNE was beginning – terrible it was – and diphtheria. So many of those diseases are gone now, thank heaven.

Gwen stopped the tape for a few minutes.

"Imagine a young woman from Toronto going out to that homestead," Olive said.

"Seems to me you went out to a ranch when you got married," Tom reminded her.

"Oh, yes, of course. But we had a car then, and running water in the house, and a Delco system for electricity, and the radio, and – oh, lots of things."

"In the next part of the tape I got Mother back to that first spring when she was pregnant," Gwen said. "Listen to this." She started the machine again, and Martha's voice filled the room.

"Well, the first thing after we got there, after the garden planting, of course, was to get the wheat into the ground. Will worked like a beaver to get twenty acres ploughed and harrowed and seeded. He borrowed a seeder from a neighbour who was already finished. [Here Martha laughed.] You know, with all that hard work, all Will could think of was how good that soil was. 'Black loam, the best soil in the world,' he would say.

"Every single seed we put into the ground grew like the dickens, so when November came and the baby was due we had a root cellar full of potatoes, carrots, beets, and parsnips. And that twenty acres! It yielded thirty bushels to the acre. Imagine! So we had six hundred bushels of wheat to sell. Even after paying for threshing we had a tidy profit.

"And then winter came.

"Tom was born on November second, on the night of our first real winter blizzard, and one of the worst we ever had. The wind howled around our poor little house and the snow drifted against it. Will had carefully banked the sides of the house with straw and earth and manure to keep out the floor drafts. And he had stuffed old pieces of wool into the cracks around the windows. The front door was permanently closed, and he put a heavy storm door over it, and tar paper over that. The back door, on the south side of the house, had a heavy storm door too. There was a good supply of wood and a scuttle of coal in to keep the range going all night.

"Daddy had sent us books and advice on all phases of childbirth. The poor man, he was worried sick because he knew all the complications that can occur. But I'll never forget that night as long as I live.

"Our neighbour, Mrs. Ferguson, was supposed to come and help, but of course because of the awful storm she couldn't. So there were just the two of us alone in that little house, with the coal-oil lamp throwing funny shadows on the wall. I'll never forget those shadows. And Will. He was wonderful. Men didn't have anything to do with childbirth then, as they do now. But you know he wasn't the least bit frightened. Of course, he'd helped cows and mares have their young, and we had all those instructions.

"We often had a good laugh about it afterwards. You see, one of the things Daddy told us was that he had to shave the area, you know, down there. So Will got his straight razor and his shaving cream and he went at it. Then when he'd just nicely got started he stopped and looked at me and said, 'Can you go like this?' And he screwed his mouth over to one side the way men do when they're shaving. Well, I burst out laughing, and you know, that helped. Relaxed me.

"And Tommy, well, you'd think he was impatient to get out into the world. He's always been impatient and energetic, wanting to get going. Well, he came easy as anything and right away started yelling his head off. Will cleaned him up and wrapped him warmly and then he made some tea."

"Tea?"

"Yes, I suddenly had a great craving for tea. Of course

I've always been a tea granny, and it was one thing we had. Gracious, I don't know what we'd have done without tea. It came in big lead-foil packages, and it would keep forever as long as you kept it dry. Whenever I felt low I drank tea. I guess that's why I wanted it then. You know, I used to wonder why in all the stories of childbirth somebody always said to have lots of boiling water ready. I learned what it was for – to make the tea!"

"Mother, you talk as though it was fun. What would you have done if there had been complications?"

"What could we do? Just the best we could, and trust in the Lord to help us. Oh, I know, people scoff at that now, but if it comes to getting help from a doctor or the Lord, I'll take the Lord every time.

"You know, dear, people sometimes ask me why I do so much church work now. Well, I think it's because I owe. You see, there were so many bad things that could have happened to us. One neighbour lost three babies, one right after the other. Just died before they were two years old. Not a blessed thing she could do about it but pray."

"But prayer didn't save her babies, Mother."

"Now don't you try getting me into some kind of philosophical argument about prayer. I don't know if it helped us or not. But none of my babies died. You may say that prayer didn't help us, but I believe it did.

"Anyway, when I awakened the next morning with my baby tucked under the feather comforter beside me, the wind had dropped and the sun was shining low on the horizon. From my bed I could see miles of white gleaming snow and flocks of snow buntings in undulating flight. It just seemed as though the Lord was smiling on us and our son. I knew then that Tommy would have a good life.

"Will was so proud. 'I had a good notion you were a remarkable woman, Martha,' he said. 'And now I'm certain of it. Well,' and he grinned, 'I must get about the chores. That cow won't milk herself, and we've got three to feed now.'

"Mrs. Ferguson arrived on a stone-boat pulled by a shaggy Clyde and announced that she would take over for the day.

" 'But what about your own man?' I asked.

" 'He can fend for himself. Do him good. A man who can't cook his own meals isn't worth having.'

"She came every day for a week and then Will and I were able to manage by ourselves. I guess I was just a natural mother, the kind of woman who is incomplete without children. I picked up my baby every chance I got and held him and kissed him and talked and sang to him all the time. I would go about my housework and tell him stories as he lay in the little crib Will had made from an apple box. And soon the baby laughed and cooed and followed me with his eyes.

"People think living alone on the bald prairie was all hardships, Gwen. Fiddlesticks. We had everything we wanted and each other and our little boy. Of course we worked hard, but gracious, we were young. The first years of a woman's marriage are always the best, and I look back on that year with nothing but happiness. Mostly I had a kind and loving man, and that makes up for everything.

"That first Christmas was the hardest time. I had never been away from my family at Christmas. We had no phone to call them, as people do now. But I fixed up the house as best I could. Will found a grove of spruce and cut a little tree and we killed our biggest rooster, and Mother had sent a lot of nuts and candy and presents. I think I missed the music most. We had no gramophone then, nor piano. But we managed by singing some carols.

"The winter was long, but not terribly much snow that year, and then spring came. Oh, my, you can never appreciate spring if you haven't lived in a homestead shack. Just to get outside without bundling up so. And the sound of the melting snow dripping off the roof and the long icicles hanging from every eave. And the smell of the earth, oh, the smell of the earth. And the prairie meadowlarks singing from the fence posts."

"Did you ever get to town in the winter?"

"Saturdays. That was the time when we always went to town. We went in the sleigh box. Everybody did. The stores were open until late and it was a time for shopping, and for visiting and getting the local news. Whose child had the measles, whose sow had had pigs. And the railway station."

"The railway station?"

"Yes, the railway was everything to us, our link with the outside world. Almost everything we bought came by rail and everything we sold went away by rail. And the mail, of course, and the magazines we got from Toronto, *Saturday Night* and others. Gracious, everybody went to the station. We'd stand together on that long wooden platform talking to friends, exchanging gossip and recipes, and then we'd hear it away off, that eerie cry of the steam whistle. Little children would get down and put their ears to the rails, if we'd let them. Not ours, of course, but some of the more daring ones, like the Rafter children. There were ten of them and they seemed to be everywhere without supervision. Mr. Rafter did odd jobs around the town and one of these was to listen to the radio every noon and get the grain prices. The elevator people paid him a little for this. Oh, that train! It came in at six sharp, and we'd wait for the mail to be sorted.

"And sometimes on Saturday nights there would be skating carnivals. Skating was a big thing for us then, that and curling. We had a closed-in rink in town and of course Will and I loved to skate. After all, that's how we met, wasn't it? Oh, those carnivals. Once I put brown stuff on my face and dressed as an Indian squaw – "

"Mother!"

"What's the matter, dear?"

"Nobody uses that word to speak of Indian women any more."

"Why not, pray? It's a perfectly good word. I looked it up in the Oxford dictionary."

"But it's racist."

"Fiddlesticks. I never had anything against Indians, even if they were a lazy, shiftless lot. Anyway, I dressed up like this Indian ... woman ... and nobody knew me. Not even Will. We had such a laugh. He actually skated with me, on a dare from some of the other men, and the things he said! Well, we certainly had a laugh about that! Will didn't laugh much, though.

"Those skating carnivals were fun, but then of course I got pregnant and that was the end of skating for a while. Daddy was cross about me getting pregnant so often and so soon, but my goodness, what could we do about it? Anyway, each baby was as welcome as the one before. And Mother sent so many things for the babies that we couldn't possibly use them all and so we gave them away to neighbours. They were glad enough to get them."

"What did you do for baby-sitters?"

"Never heard of them. We took the children everywhere. To the rink, to dances, everywhere. There was always a grandmother sitting along the side of the dance floor and you could just plunk a baby on her lap. And the children danced just as we did. So the winters weren't all bad.

"During the hot summer days when the crops were growing, Will loved to build. Pigpens, granaries, additions to the house and barn. When he had nothing to build at home he'd help a neighbour. 'You know,' he told me, 'if we ever leave this farm I'm going to get into the construction business.'

"When the war broke out in Europe in 1914 many of the young men from the prairies went off to be butchered in a cause they didn't understand. Will made his decision. 'I'd be no earthly good to them,' he said. 'Don't know one end of a gun from the other, and I don't think I could ever kill anyone. So I'll stay here and raise kids and grain so there'll be something for those boys to come home to.'

"And that's what he did. Hugh and Alvin were born during the war. The price of wheat rose and farmers did well. As the war dragged on and the casualty lists included local boys, there were incidents in town. In the grocery store the wife of the lumber dealer, who had been one of the first to leave, made a remark about 'those cowards who stayed home.' Well, I marched over to her, planted myself squarely in front of her, and said, 'Your man went to war because he wanted to. Mine stayed home because he wanted to. I'm not sure why some men want to go away and others don't, but I think maybe their wives have something to do with it.' Since the lumber dealer was a well-known womanizer who made frequent trips to Regina and boasted about his amorous adventures there, most of the listeners were on my side.

"By the time the war was over, Will was farming a section and a half of land, mostly by himself because hired men were hard to find. He had enlarged and improved the house and built a new barn. He had eight good horses and a pair of spirited drivers. His good fortune came about in 1916, when he sowed most of his land to flax. He had a good crop and the price was high. Many of the new houses on the prairies were built with profits from flax.

"Then in 1922 we made up our minds to leave the farm. We needed better schools for the children, and I wanted to be able to walk to church and join a library and go to some plays and movies.

"The post-war boom was in full swing, and after four years of idleness, building was in great demand. We decided to move to Saskatoon.

"And again luck was in our corner. Will actually

made arrangements to sell the farm, but the deal fell through. A man who'd come back from the war and had no capital wanted to rent it, so Will let him have it. We never did sell it. And the wonderful thing was that, although we didn't know it, we owned the mineral rights to the land. Now who would have ever thought of finding minerals on the prairie? But minerals included oil, and oil was found there in 1948. 'Just luck,' Will said. 'Blind, stupid luck!'

"So I became a city woman again, and our farming days were over. Will formed a construction firm and, operating mostly on credit, began building houses. Whole streets of houses.

"The Roaring Twenties, they call them now. I had my hair bobbed. When Will saw it I thought he'd have a fit. But he got used to it.

"I had four children and soon would have one more, but we had the advantage of electricity. Electricity, that great emancipator of women. It washed the clothes, ironed the clothes, cooked the meals, heated the curling irons that had been heated by sticking them down into lamp chimneys. It vacuumed the rugs and, most important of all, it lit every corner of the house.

"And running water! You never realize the advantages of running water unless you've been running to fetch it for years. Turn a tap and there it is. Hot and cold. Take a hot bath whenever you feel like it, and I loved baths. Go to the privy in the rain and never wet your feet. We lived in an apartment until Will got the house built. Big, spacious house that was as much like the house in Rosedale as I could remember it.

"Oh, it was a good time for us. I became a member of the library board and launched a campaign to have it enlarged. We wouldn't have shelf space for Eugene O'Neill or Hemingway unless we got rid of some Hardy or Dickens. And we couldn't do that. We needed them all. I joined the theatre guild and the Kinnets and worked for the Red Cross. Usually at meetings I had a baby in my arms and a toddler by the hand. But it was easy. You see, I had no chores. Besides, Tom and Hugh were in school by then.

"And we had two cars. I had a new Essex coupe, and of course Will had that peppy little Model A pick-up truck. He roared from job to job from early morning until late at night. My goodness, how that man worked. And he was happier than I'd ever seen him. He was so optimistic. Of course everybody was. Why, it was so easy to make money and so easy to get credit. Oh, yes, easy to get credit. Everything Will did he did on credit. We really didn't own anything, not the house, not the cars. Will owed the lumber yards and the hardware for nails and, oh, everything.

"Oh, dear, it was horrible when the crash came. We were wiped out. Everybody who'd been so willing to give credit and lend money wanted it back right away. The bank held a mortgage on the house and they took it from us. My dear little car went, and the truck, and all the lots Will had made down payments on. Gone.

"One of Will's friends in the same business just loaded his family and clothes into a car and drove off leaving everything. But we didn't do that.

"Wiped out completely. There was no hope from home. Like a lot of doctors, Daddy had been in the stock market up to his ears and lost all his investments. So there we were, five children and no money. Have you any idea what it means to have no money? I don't mean no ready cash, or an overdrawn bank account, I mean rock-bottom, flat broke. I tell you, it's awful!"

"I remember. I was seven years old. We moved from the big house into that little shack on Elm Street."

"Indeed we did. The rent was ten dollars a month. Will tried so hard to get a job. He tried selling encyclopaedias from door to door, but nobody had any money for books. Then he tried selling insurance. He sold a few policies to friends, but that soon dried up. He even tried selling funeral plots. That poor man. He'd pore over the help-wanted ads and trudge the streets answering them. But there were always others there ahead of him.

"Tom had a job in a grocery store. That poor kid. All he got for pay at the end of the week was a receipt for the groceries he'd fetched home. But, you know, he never complained. Not Tom. Hugh wanted to quit school, too, but we wouldn't let him. Oh, dear, it was such an awful time. And Alvin. Oh, I can't talk about Alvin.

"We even thought of going back to the farm, but with the drought and grasshoppers and dust storms, and the price of wheat down to thirty-five cents a bushel, there was no point in that. Besides, I'd had enough of farms.

"Then we got a bright idea.

" 'What about your marmalade?' Will said. 'You make the best marmalade in Canada. Not sugar-sweet like the store-bought junk, but with a hint of bitterness. You've been making it for years and giving it away. Maybe we could sell it.'

" 'Why not?' I said. 'Everybody says it's the best marmalade they ever tasted in their lives. I have all the equipment. I've got lots of jars and enough sugar for one batch.'

"And so we made marmalade and sold it door to door for thirty-five cents a jar. In no time we were selling it as fast as we could make it. At first Will delivered it; then we recruited Hugh and Alvin to work after school. I began sewing fancy little aprons, which Will also sold. But there was no repeat business, except for presents. Unlike a jar of marmalade, an apron would last a long time.

"And so, with what Tom was able to earn and what Hugh sent home after he went teaching, we managed to get through the Depression without ever having to take relief.

"But the Depression left its mark on the entire family. Never again would any of us go into debt. Never would we take good fortune for granted and never would we be able to spend money lavishly. We were and always would be 'Depression-minded.'

"Well, you know the rest of the story as well as I do. War broke out in September of 1939 and that ended the Depression. And, mysteriously, the rains began to fall. Will got a job almost right away. There were lots of jobs then. And all those unemployed young men and a lot that had jobs joined the armed forces. Good times again. Isn't it awful that it had to be a war that brought the good times. And if only Alvin hadn't. . . . [Here Martha began to cry quietly.] I'm sorry, Gwen, but I don't want to talk any more.

When the tape recorder was shut off, the brothers and sisters sat silent.

Chapter Nine

Hugh Windmar sat on a knoll of the river bank where he had played as a boy. He was surrounded by saskatoon berry bushes, chokecherry bushes, and birch trees that he was beginning to remember. For, gradually, after listening to his parents' tapes he was being dragged back into the past, a past that he had tried to avoid thinking about for almost half a century.

He was beginning to realize that he was home. All the way home. The place that, like it or not, had helped to shape him, that had filled him with the resentment and the frustration that were part of his drive. A drive that had brought him to the top of his profession. "We are what we have been," he muttered to himself, as boyhood memories began to fill his mind.

His most vivid memories were of Saskatoon. He remembered little about the homestead. Mostly tagging along after Tom when Tom went out to drive the cows home to be milked. Usually they came by themselves with their bags so full they waddled, but there was always Daisy, the wayward one, who was reluctant to follow the others. So Tom and the farm collie, Gyp, had to go out and steer her to the barnyard, and Hugh would tag along behind.

When they moved to Saskatoon, Hugh tagged after Tom to Queen Mary School. Tom was in grade three by that time and, although he didn't care much for school, he got along well, making up for his lack of scholarship with a winning, outgoing disposition. He matured early and by the time he was in grade eight he was a tall, handsome boy with an easy-going manner and a broad, friendly smile.

He was also a natural athlete and captain of the hockey and baseball teams at school. He became something of a hero to boys and girls alike.

"Squirt." He could still hear his brother laughing at him when he tried to field a grounder at third base. "For Chrissake, Squirt. With your hands, not your feet!" Tom was never mean or cruel, just thoughtless. He never knew how much it hurt to be laughed at.

But the worst memory involving Tom was the game of slugs. This was one of those useless, completely ridiculous games that boys often play. It happened one cold winter night when Hugh and Tom and Jimmy Field were playing road-apple hockey under a corner street lamp. Jimmy's father ran the neighbourhood grocery store, and he bribed other kids with candy and cigarettes. The rink was the hard-packed snow of the road, their puck a frozen horse turd. Two tin cans were set up at each end to mark the goals. Since few cars were on the road in winter then, their game was seldom interrupted.

Jimmy and Hugh were teamed up against Tom, but even together they were no match for the faster, older boy. Jimmy got tired of the game and wanted to entice Tom into his house where he could have him all to himself. This often happened: Jimmy was Hugh's best friend except when Tom was around. He managed to whisper to Tom that his folks were out and there was a bottle of cooking sherry they could get into.

"I've got a headache," Tom announced. "Think I'll go home."

"Me, too," Jimmy said.

Hugh was furious. "You can't quit now when you're ahead," he shouted. "That's cheating."

"Okay, you little squirt. We'll play until you catch up."

So the game became more of a battle than a contest, and Hugh grew more and more angry. Then, when he and Tom were battling for the puck, Tom slugged Hugh's stick.

"Okay, okay, okay," Hugh screamed. "So you want a game of slugs."

This meant that one boy would hold his hockey stick

blade down while the other boy slugged it. They would take turns until one of their sticks was broken. As it happened, Tom had a brand new Mart Hooper stick that he'd got by saving up the cards from hockey bars. It was his pride and joy. Hugh's stick, on the other hand, was an old, gnarled thing he'd had for months, tough as iron.

"Think I'm crazy?" Tom scoffed. "Slug against that junk of yours?"

"You're afraid," Hugh screamed. "Yellow, yellow, yellow!"

Of course no boy could take this, especially Tom. "Okay," he said. "Hold your gawdamned stick."

Hugh did and Tom slugged it half-heartedly.

"Now it's my turn." Hugh was almost crying.

Tom held his stick out. Hugh, crazed with anger and humiliation, brought his old club down on it with all his strength. The lovely new stick shattered in two pieces.

"Satisfied, you miserable little fart?" Tom shouted and threw the broken halves of his stick off into a snow bank. "Come on, Jimmy, let's go."

The two of them left for Jimmy's house while Hugh stood alone in the cold crisp air, under the feeble glare of the street lamp, tears of rage freezing on his cheeks. Even now the memory of it made him wince. Somehow it summed up one part of their relationship. The bad part.

Tom quit school after grade eight and went to work as a carpenter's helper in his father's contracting business. He had a quick mind and natural mechanical skills and soon became a master carpenter. He began to think about a contracting business of his own.

Everything was booming in those last years of the 1920s. Anybody could make money and most people who made it invested it in the stock market. Why, you didn't even need much money to invest. It was done on the instalment plan, or margin. Long before the instalment came due the stock had doubled or tripled, so you sold it and invested the money in still more stock or margin. It was a wonderful, heady time.

Hugh wrote his grade-eight departmental exams when he was still very young, having skipped a couple of grades along the way, and graduated with the highest marks in his class. He won the IODE award for history and the prize was a book called *Under Haig in Flanders*. It was all about the Great War and the bravery of the Canadians. He didn't like it.

When Hugh went off to the Gardner Collegiate Institute, he was younger than the other boys in his class and quite a bit smaller. He resented this. He also resented the fact that most of the boys were better at hockey and baseball than he was, and were open and free with the girls. He seemed like a shy, timid boy, but he was full of fire and sex drive and especially resentment.

So Hugh concentrated on what he could do better than the others. The high-school course of those days was as difficult as most university courses today. There was Latin and French and physics and chemistry and the entire history of Europe. And at every level there were exams that came from the department of education in Regina in sealed envelopes. And the students' written answers were sealed in big envelopes that didn't have names on them, which in turn were sent off to Regina to be marked. Each year Hugh was at the head of his class and gathered in medals and prizes.

Hugh turned fourteen, a most disturbing age for any young man. He was feeling the drive of sex and couldn't control it; his nights were plagued with wet dreams and most of his waking hours filled with wild sex fantasies. No one had bothered to warn him of what was going to happen to him, and so he was completely unprepared. His parents and teachers grinned smugly at the change in his voice, but that was all.

His natural shyness was enhanced by his condition, and his feelings of shame and guilt were intense. He concentrated on his studies and his writing, and often when he lay awake at night he would pray that he would not have shameful dreams where he performed shameful acts. Years later, he often wondered about the colossal stupidity and insensitivity of those times. It was the age of hypocrisy.

In the late twenties people were greedy and naïve, and men with no talent for business believed that they could become rich by investing in the stock market, and that what went up would never come down.

Then on Thursday, October 24, 1929, Hugh's existence was abruptly shattered. The effect on the family was varied. Tom, a born survivor, survived. When his job with William Henry's company disappeared he managed to get another, delivering for a grocery store. Alvin, who was eleven, was in grade four and so felt little effect of his parents' poverty. Olive and Gwen were nine and seven years old; they still played their skipping games on the street and sang their songs. Martha kept them as well-dressed as any children in school.

Hugh suffered the most. He resented their poverty. Each evening after school he would load up a box of marmalade jars, put them on a sleigh, and tramp through the dark, cold streets calling at houses, carefully avoiding those of his classmates, asking people to buy marmalade. On alternate nights he took a basket filled with aprons his mother had made and offered them for sale. Although he was not a natural salesman, he was a good actor. Gradually he learned the key words that would most affect his audience, and after a month or so he was selling marmalade as fast as his parents could make it.

"Good experience for you," his father assured him. "You don't learn anything from prosperity. It's adversity that builds character."

Often it was seven or eight o'clock before he got home, tired, cold, and hungry. Martha always kept his supper warm for him.

Hugh worked even harder at school and turned into a bitter and determined rebel. He became editor of the school newspaper and wrote cantankerous, sarcastic articles about the academic program and the sports program and anything else he disagreed with.

And he was feisty and critical in class, asking teachers questions they couldn't answer and disagreeing with their opinions. Because of his academic excellence, they could do little about it.

On one occasion he asked a math teacher about the value of the binomial theorem. The teacher, a bit of a wag, replied that, if nothing else, you could dazzle a stranger on the street by reciting it. This brought laughter from the class and a flush of anger to Hugh's cheeks. He rushed to his typewriter and dashed off an article called "Academic Nonsense," a scathing criticism of the school's entire program. He didn't hesitate to name the math teacher and hold him up to even greater ridicule than Hugh had suffered in class.

This caused a furore throughout the staff, and there was a lot of talk about freedom of the press and students' rights; there was also an examination of the school curriculum. Hugh experienced the excitement and delight of ruffling sacred feathers. His career as a writer was determined with that article. He could hardly wait to get into university, where he knew there would be more and better targets for his vitriolic pen.

And he became an active pacifist. The great cry of intellectuals of the twenties was that war was a crime against humanity and as such should be outlawed. He read avidly the works of Bernard Shaw and Bertrand Russell, quoting them fulsomely in his own writing. His particular target was the ROTC, as the young officers' training corps was called. He dubbed it the Ridiculous Order of Termagant Churls.

And he learned about the power of the pen. For although his classmates and teachers might not like his jibes, they stood in awe of him. Teachers, he realized, could not come down hard on the best student in the school. To do so would be to deny their steadfast belief that character and worth and honesty and genuine all-round goodness could be gauged by the marks on an exam paper.

But although he earned for himself a position of eminence as a student, writer, debater, public speaker, and wit, socially he was a flop. He seemed always to be saying the wrong things to girls. He tried to be funny and friendly, but it always came out wrong. Mostly this was because when he got within two feet of an attractive or sexy girl – and all high-school girls are sexy – her presence, her essence so aroused him that he became a blubbering boob.

How he yearned to be free and easy with girls, and go to their parties and dance and neck and play parlour games like post office, but he just couldn't. He was invited to a few parties, but he made such an ass of himself that he wasn't asked again.

Martha, who was naturally gregarious and fun-loving, was continually urging him to have a party, but he always found some excuse not to. Besides, most of the girls he coveted were taller than he was.

Oh, there were girls who had the reputation of being available and were the subjects of ribald conversation in the locker room before gym classes, but he wanted none of them. For he was in his religious phase and fervently believed that smoking and drinking and fornication were heinous sins for which he would be punished with cancer or venereal disease or worse.

The plain fact was that for all his bravado and attempted sophistication he was frightened, insecure, and shy.

His father's opinion was that he took himself too seriously. His mother said he was an idealist. Tom said he just needed a change of oil.

"What does that mean?" Hugh asked.

"Have you ever screwed a girl?"

"God, but you are gauche!"

"I don't know what that means, little brother, but I do know that a good roll in the hay would do wonders for you. Clear up your pimples."

"I don't know any girls like that."

"They are all like that. Take it from one who knows. They all want the same thing. Some know they want it, others don't. Takes a little longer with that kind."

"I suppose you know all about it."

"I wrote the book. Listen, I'll lend you my car. Pick out

the hottest number in your class. Oh, don't get me wrong, I mean a nice girl. Take her to the movies and then drive out to a place I know on the river bank. Take some rum along. Nothing like a little booze to get the motor started. Pour an ounce or so into a bottle of Coke and then recap it. You get out there under the moon and just casually let your arm drop over her shoulder and let your hand move down to her breast, then see what happens."

"You are a bastard, you know that? A real bastard!"

"Okay, okay. But you just try it. Look, I know you get the urges. I've heard you panting and puffing in the bathroom."

"You bastard!"

"Look, there's nothing wrong with it, as long as you don't overdo it. Won't grow hair on the palms of your hands or make you sick. Certain amount is good for you, but believe me, brother, it doesn't compare with the real thing."

Hugh knew he was right. Just talking about it aroused him. "But what about pregnancy or disease?"

"Wear a rubber. Be sure and do that. You get so hot you forget to put it on and you could be in a lot of trouble. It's like washing your hands with gloves on, but it's better than nothing."

"Where do I get this rubber?"

"Any drugstore. Listen, I've got some. Keep them in my extra shoes so Ma won't find them. Help yourself."

"Oh, go to hell," Hugh said, and Tom laughed.

But Hugh thought about it; in fact, he couldn't stop thinking about it. It went dead against all his Sunday school and boys' club teachings, but, well, if it were for health reasons. . . .

Then one day he found himself alone in the cloakroom with Elvira Mercy and she smiled at him, and before he knew it he had asked her for a date.

She looked at him quizzically and said, "Why yes, I would like that. John Gilbert and Greta Garbo are on at the Daylight this weekend. Could we go to that?"

"Sure could," he said. Gosh, it had been easy.

At noon he asked Tom about the car and Tom said, "Sure, little brother. Just happens I was planning to stay in anyway. Uh, don't forget the rubber and the Coke."

Afterwards Hugh thought that if he'd had a normal, easy relationship with girls he wouldn't have done what he did. As it was, he almost didn't do it at all, but just before he was about to go out the door on Friday night, Tom stopped him and handed him two bottles of Coke and a small envelope.

"Go ahead," he urged when Hugh demurred. "You may never use them but, as the Boy Scouts say, it never hurts to be prepared." He slipped the envelope into Hugh's pocket.

Hugh took the two Cokes and the car keys and left. He put the Cokes in the glove compartment of the Buick coupe and drove down to Starlight Boulevard and parked in front of Elvira's house.

He sat there, fingering the knob on the gear shift and cursing himself roundly. Damn it all to hell, why couldn't he be like other fellows? Why couldn't he just go in and talk easily and wittily to Elvira and her parents? Why was he sweating and why was his heart thumping just at the thought of being close to her?

Finally he got out and walked up to the front door. He rang the bell and nothing happened. He was just about to ring it again when it was opened by a tall bald man with glasses, oozing prosperity and self-assurance.

"Well," he said.

Why in hell did he have to say that as though he was about to address a prisoner in the dock? Mr. Mercy was a judge. He was also tall and prosperous, the things that brought out the worst in Hugh.

"Well," he said from somewhere above Hugh's head. "You must be Hugh Windmar. Elvira has told us about you."

Told them about him. Sounded like, "We're on to you. You have no secrets here." Hugh thought of the Coke bottles in the glove compartment and the little rubber circle burning a hole in his shirt pocket. He pulled his jacket straight in front, but couldn't think of a thing to say. He felt like the gawky kid in Eugene O'Neill's *Ah Wilderness*, awkward, shy, tongue-tied, and altogether stupid.

"Come in, come in," the judge said. "Sit down. Elvira will be right down."

Hugh sat in the big plush chair. He felt as though his feet barely reached the floor.

The judge said, "I hear you're quite a writer."

"Yes, sir. I mean, well, I'm the editor of the school paper."

"I've read some of your stuff."

"You have?"

"Oh, yes, Elvira brings the paper home every Friday. Very interesting, your views on the educational system. Tell me, what do you mean by saying that it's ninety per cent propaganda?"

"Well, isn't it?"

"Young man, it is natural at your age to be a critic of the educational system, the political system, religious institutions. I know that. But you must remember that these systems, although far from perfect, have worked well."

"Worked for whom?" Damn. He hadn't meant to get into an argument, especially with a judge, the personification of the status quo. Luckily, Elvira came down the stairs then and all thought fled from his mind.

"I'm ready." God, she looked like Norma Shearer, and Hugh had been in love with Norma Shearer since he began going to movies.

The judge kissed her on the cheek and shook hands with Hugh.

"I'd like to continue our discussion some other time," he said.

Hugh nodded and followed Elvira out the door. He opened the right door of the coupe and closed it behind her. Then he went around and got in behind the wheel. It was all very cosy, except that damned judge seemed to be sitting there between them.

"Where are we going?' she asked.

"Well, I thought maybe the Daylight, as you suggested. Greta Garbo and John Gilbert?"

She laughed. "Oh, no. Greta Garbo is far too much competition for me. There's such a good moon tonight. Let's drive down to Lovers' Ridge and watch it over the river and, well, just talk."

"Lovers' Ridge? You know about that?"

"Doesn't everybody?"

"Yeah, yeah, of course, but there are other people there. I know a better place."

"You do? My . . . I've misjudged you."

"My brother told me about it."

"Oh? Tell me about your brother."

"Well, he's two years older than I am. And about half a foot taller and he's good at just about everything."

"Does he go to university?" She was definitely interested in university students.

"No, he works for Dad in the construction business," he lied. "But who wants to talk about him?"

"Not me. Drive on, James, to that secluded rendezvous."

So he drove out past the university and down a narrow rutted road to the brow of a cliff looking over the river. There were no other cars there. Below them the Saskatchewan River, more than a quarter of a mile wide, flowed north. The full moon was reflected in the water.

"Isn't this better than any old movie?" Elvira, the judge's daughter, cooed and cuddled up close to him.

She took his right arm and pulled it around her shoulder, and sure enough his hand came right down to her breast. But he couldn't bring himself to press that soft, warm bulge.

"Are you as shy as they say you are?" she asked.

"Of course not. Actually there is no such thing as shyness. You see, according to Freud – "

She put her dainty little finger on his mouth and said, "Then kiss me."

So he kissed her on the lips and it was the first time he had ever kissed a woman. His penis was so stiff it was hurting him.

She kissed him and he could feel her little tongue against his, and he almost went off in his pants.

Then, without removing her lips from his, she took his right hand and moved it gently down inside her dress to her bare breast.

He shifted in the seat and brought his other hand around to her thigh and when she squirmed against him he moved it up to her crotch. Yes, it was there all right, just as he'd seen in pictures, and it was warm and soft and covered with soft hair. He pressed against it and felt his finger enter. The feel of it almost drove him crazy. He thrust farther and harder.

"Stop it, Hughie!" she protested. "You're hurting me!"

But he couldn't stop. She reached down and pulled his hand away. He tore at her panties and felt something rip.

"Stop, Hughie! What's the matter with you?"

He didn't stop. Tried to shift his legs over on top of her and at the same time unbutton his pants. But the front seat of a Buick coupe was hardly intended for such manoeuvres. As he lurched over, the knob of the gear shift dealt him a cruel blow on the testicle and he cried out with pain. But he kept on and squeezed her into the corner of the seat.

He managed to get his pants unbuttoned, but his rigid penis was hard against his stomach and far above the fly of his shorts. He tried to get his shorts down, but it wasn't easy; the elastic caught on the end of his penis. Then he got his hand on it, but that was too much for his poor aching, throbbing organ and the semen shot out of it like water from a hose all over his pants and Elvira's dress.

She had yelled for him to stop and was almost screaming when the mess hit her.

"Now look what you've done! All over my dress! Honestly, Hughie, you are the worst boy I've ever been out with in my whole life. You've torn my panties and ruined my dress. What will I tell my mother?"

But Hugh was in no condition to answer. He was sitting on his own side of the seat, panting and relieved, but so ashamed of himself that he could scarcely breathe.

"I'm sorry, Elvira. Gosh, I'm sorry." He began frantically

rubbing at her dress with his handkerchief.

"Stop it," she screamed. "Leave me alone. You tried to rape me!"

"Rape! No, no . . . honestly. It never entered my head. You wouldn't tell anyone that!"

"If I did, my father would kill you or have you put in jail where you belong!"

"Oh, God!"

"Take me home. Right now. Take me home!"

So he started the Buick and drove out the rutted dirt road and through the university grounds and down Shaw Street to Starlight Boulevard. He stopped in front of her house. It was dark.

"Maybe your folks are out," he said.

"Lucky for you if they are."

"Uh . . . can I come in with you?"

"What? And finish what you started? I don't know what kind of a girl you thought you were out with. Honestly. I never want to go out with you again, or even speak to you, or see you if I can help it."

All this last was said as she wrenched open the door of the Buick. Then, holding her soiled dress away from her so the vile stuff wouldn't pollute her sweet young body, she ran up the walk and into the house.

Hugh drove home feeling so low that for one wild moment he thought of driving the car down the steep bank of the river and ending it all. But with his luck, he realized, the car would probably be wrecked and he wouldn't even be hurt. So he drove home, parked the car in the driveway, and hurried into the house and up to the room he shared with Tom.

He had just removed his trousers when Tom came into the room. "How'd it go, little brother? Jesus, what happened to your pants?"

"None of your goddamned business. And if you laugh at me I'll kill you!"

"I believe you would." Tom sat on the bed and didn't laugh. "Didn't go so well, eh, little brother?"

"And stop calling me little brother. Just because I happen to be a few inches shorter than you and a few years younger, must you go on humiliating me forever?"

"Humiliating? What do you mean?"

"Making fun of me. You're always making fun of me. Just because you can play ball better and hockey and everything else, including screwing!"

That did it. Tom began to laugh and Hugh couldn't help but laugh with him.

"That's not true, you know," Tom said. "Naw. It's just that you have this funny idea about women. You idealize them and you're scared of them."

Hugh looked at him in surprise, hardly expecting such prescience from his brother.

"I do?"

"Yeah. You got too many brains for your own good in some ways. Makes you take things too seriously."

"But you said they all wanted it."

"Yeah, yeah, but that was – well, it was a mistake for me to say that. I gave you a bum steer. Those little high-school twirps are all talk and no action. Cock-teasers, that's what they are. Go right along with everything but the real thing."

"Yeah. She said I tried to rape her. God, if she tells her father that. . . ."

"She won't tell her old man that, not in a million years. Proving rape against a guy that you went out in the car alone with to the river bank is impossible. A good lawyer would tear her to pieces. And her old man, the judge, would know it."

"I hope so."

"Forget that little skirt. What you need is a real woman. I can introduce you to one."

"A whore? No, thanks."

"There you go. Thinking there's only two kinds, nice girls and whores. Well, you're dead wrong. There are a lot of women who are honest and decent and clean and all the things you think those high-school girls are, but – "

"They screw?"

"Oh, God, there you go. They make love. They're just generous, loving women. This one I'm talking about will make you feel like a million dollars."

"What does she do, this perfect woman?"

"Well, as a matter of fact, she's married."

"Married!"

"Yeah. Husband's a local politician. You'd be surprised if I told you his name, but he's so goddamned busy with meetings and chasing votes and other women he hasn't got much time for his wife."

"No thanks."

"Now – "

"I don't want anything to do with this kind, clean woman of yours who screws for the fun of it. No, I'll find a woman of my own some day. A decent woman who is a virgin."

"A virgin! You mean somebody under six years old. That's all the virgins there are around."

"No, you're wrong. I know you're wrong."

"Okay, okay. Maybe I am. But when you meet this perfect virgin, don't scare her off. Just do what comes naturally." He got up. "Jesus, I gotta go. Heavy date."

He left the room and Hugh felt better.

When Hugh graduated from high school, he was glad to get out of the place.

"The thing to do now," his English teacher assured him, "is to go on to university. Don't put it off. I know some young people think they can work a year or so and then go, but in the meantime they get married and there go their careers."

He didn't say how Hugh was to raise the money for university. There were no jobs to be had, even if he had wanted one. So while other members of his class, some with barely enough marks to pass, went to university, Hugh went to the provincial normal school.

His mother was determined that he go. Being a schoolteacher held a certain status for her, although teachers were working for starvation wages. Somehow she managed to save the twenty-five dollars needed for his tuition, and then Hugh got a break. A boy he knew who had a paper route was willing to sell it. Hugh bought it for his first week's pay, and instead of trudging through the streets selling marmalade, he trudged through the streets delivering papers. And thus it came about that, as he often boasted, he went from paper-boy to school principal in one year.

Chapter Ten

"I got an idea," Tom said to his brothers and sisters the next day. They were playing croquet on the lawn.

"Let's hear it," Olive said. "I'm sick of this game. Croquet was never meant for the Windmar family. Too many ways to make each other mad. We can think of things to fight over besides whamming each others' balls into the shrubbery."

"You miss the point of the game," Gwen said.

"Explain it to me, sister dear. You know everything about everything."

"Hey, cut it out, you two," Hugh said. It was ever thus, he thought. Those two will never get along. "What's your great idea, Tom?"

"Let's all go out to the Forestry Farm and have a picnic. Just like we used to do back in the twenties."

"I'm for that," Shawn said. "I'm too good at this game for you seniors, anyway."

The Forestry Farm, Hugh thought. An oasis of greenery on the barren prairie. An experimental farm where the Department of Agriculture tried out plants and fruits. Great green lawns surrounded by flowers and shrubbery. Gad, the picnics. Running races where Tom always beat him. And the girls with their hair flying, and Alvin, wiry and quick as a cat.

"Mother won't want to join us," Olive said. "I've tried to get her to go, often, but she says it reminds her of Alvin and then she starts to cry."

There it is, Hugh thought. Alvin, whose memory hangs

over this family like a thundercloud. Why should they all feel guilty about him? Just because he suffered more during the Depression than any of us. And the war. That rotten, stinking war.

"How about you, brother?" Tom broke in on his thoughts. "Forestry Farm?"

"No, I think I'll go in and talk to Mother. Haven't had a chance, really." He started towards the door.

"Well, well, imagine that," he heard Olive say. "Showing some interest in the family after all."

Hugh found his mother in her upstairs sitting room where she spent a good deal of her time. She was sewing a dress for one of her many grandchildren. He stood in the doorway watching her before she noticed him. She looked tired and frail and it came to him that after he left he would never see her alive again.

"Mother," he said softly.

She looked up with her radiant smile. "Well, Hughie. Come in, dear. Sit down and tell me about yourself."

"Nothing much to tell. I've been lucky. Luckier than most. Alvin, for instance."

"Oh, Alvin." Her hand went to her mouth.

"Please. It might help to talk about him."

"Maybe. Do you know that I never cried when the telegram came. Will did, but I couldn't. Oh, that stupid war, that terribly stupid war. Alvin always hated the idea of war. He never had a chance. The Depression and then the war."

"Tell me about Alvin, Mother. Please. He was born on the homestead, wasn't he?"

"Yes. And such a hard time we had. It was as though he didn't want to enter the world at all. He almost didn't. I'm sure neither of us would have survived if it hadn't been for Mrs. Ferguson, our neighbour. The word had a different meaning then, on the homestead. Not like a next-door neighbour you have a nodding acquaintance with. The Fergusons lived two miles away, on the next section, and we couldn't have got along without them. Busy as she was, she stayed right there with me all day and all night. She knew what to do."

"And the doctor?"

"There was still no doctor in Edenvale. The nearest one was nearly thirty miles away. And no way for him to get to us. The roads were all snowed in. Will couldn't go for him. He had to stay and keep the fires up and look after Tom and Hugh. And there was the milking and other chores that I usually did." She sighed, thinking of it. "Oh, that homestead!"

Hugh had heard the rest of the story, both from Alvin and Tom. Alvin had been a puny child and he cried a lot. Martha didn't have enough milk for him and he was always hungry. At first he slept with his parents, then in a small crib Will made for him. With the two other boys always underfoot, Martha had little time for the baby, but somehow she managed to keep that little shack of a house spotlessly clean and her children clean as well. It meant a lot of scrubbing of floors and clothes, but she did it.

When spring finally came she was able to set the baby outside in the sun with Tom to watch him. Even at six years of age Tom was responsible, a characteristic he maintained throughout his life.

Not so Hugh, who always resented the new baby taking his place in Martha's arms. Not that he would ever harm the baby, but he did like to make him cry. When Alvin began to toddle the Christmas after he was born, it was surprising how many times he tripped over one of Hugh's feet.

That was the year the soldiers came home from the war, bringing with them the terrible influenza epidemic that wiped out entire families. Will and Martha were protected by their isolation: no one in the Windmar family got the flu. But both Mrs. Ferguson and her husband died of it, leaving three children. They would be taken care of by a sister in Ontario.

As Alvin grew older he became tough and resourceful. But he was a solitary child, preferring the company of kittens and puppies to that of his brothers. At least they didn't tease or boss him. After the family left the homestead, Alvin was full of questions about everything. He and Martha played games and recited verses and sang songs. She often said he was the first child she could really enjoy. She had no cows to milk; there were electric lights and appliances; and they had a little extra money, for Will was doing well in the construction business.

"I sometimes wished Alvin would never go to school," she said. "I guess I spoiled him rotten. But he was so cute. He would stand up on a chair and sing." Martha began to sing quietly.

"When I was down beside the sea,
A wooden spade they gave to me
To dig the sandy shore.
My holes were very like a cup
In every hole the sea came up."

At school, Alvin loved the reading and the verses and ignored the rest. Very early he began writing verses of his own and drawing pictures to illustrate them. He could spend hours watching ants at work or a robin building a nest. A perceptive third-grade teacher called him "a watcher and a listener" and predicted that, with the right circumstances, he could become a writer some day, and urged Martha to encourage him.

He was lucky. Will had no foolish ideas about how a boy should participate in all sports and be tough or manly. Will didn't understand Alvin very well, but he was wise enough to appreciate the boy's feelings and his nature. Martha encouraged him in every way and bought him books on every conceivable subject. Books of verse (he knew all A. A. Milne's poems before he was eight), books of fairy tales, adventure, and humour. Books about animals and birds and the stars and the ocean and the air. He read *The Adventures of Tom Sawyer* at twelve and *Treasure Island* and the books of Booth Tarkington.

He avoided competitive sports and loathed drill classes

and the drill teacher. At the same time, he got along well with his brothers and sisters and his classmates because he was funny and bright and generous and full of laughter. He was, as Martha said, a gentle, loving person.

The Depression had a devastating effect on him. He entered high school in 1932. He earned a little money babysitting and delivering flyers door to door. But he never had enough money to buy decent clothing. Always a loner, he became more withdrawn and spent a lot of time walking on the prairie, observing birds and wild plants.

In his senior year he developed a passion for peace movements. He joined the debating society and the Youth for Peace Club at school. He looked upon war as the ultimate evil and swore he would never take part in one.

His only close friend in his senior year was Timmy McCall. They often did their homework together; they went on long hikes on weekends, played in farmers' strawstacks, and became ardent birdwatchers. And they went on the bum together.

When Alvin graduated from high school in 1936, the Depression had not yet reached its peak in Saskatchewan. Conditions might have been improving in other parts of the world, but the prairies, beset by drought, dust storms, grasshoppers, and crop failure, were still in a hopeless condition.

Tom was working and doing fine; Hugh was teaching school in Harman and hating it; Olive and Gwen were still in school. But Alvin was launched into a society that had no place for him. And it was then he learned some hard, bitter facts. The first was that to those who were employed all the unemployed were suspect. Suspect and hated, a threat to all good, industrious, hard-working men. They received little sympathy or understanding. They were useless bums.

This realization hit Alvin like a ton of bricks. He had quit his part-time job to find full-time work. After six months of looking he still didn't have full-time work, and his old job was gone. He had no job, no money, no self-respect, no hope. His natural good nature deserted him and for the few years he had yet to live he was a bitter, resentful, angry, nihilistic youth.

Timmy McCall was in the same boat, but more confused.

"What the hell happened?" he asked on a fine spring day in 1937 as they lay on the withered grass of Buena Vista Park. "Where the hell has all the money gone?"

"The rich have it and they're hanging on to it. Somebody's making a pisspot full of dough out of this Depression."

"What about this new CCF movement? Maybe we should join that."

"That's what Hugh's so all-fired excited about. But it won't work. Takes a revolution. The people with the money and the land and the inherited wealth are never going to give it up. Only thing to do is kill them, the way they did in Russia."

"Aw, come on."

"The rich are very nice people. Polite and kind, even generous in small ways, but just you try to interfere with their right to own everything and they become vicious dogs. Look at the Regina riot, if you want an example. And old Iron-heel Bennett, our millionaire ex-prime minister."

"That son of a bitch."

"They control the cops and the army and the legal system. Only way is to take it all away from them by force."

Timmy was getting uneasy. "How are things at home?" he asked.

"Terrible. I get into arguments with Dad and Tom. Tom says as soon as I get a job I'll become a capitalist like the rest of them. Shit. How are they at your place?"

"Worse. My old man called me a free-loader. If I ever talked the way you're talking he'd kick my ass out of there fast."

"Let's leave."

"Where? How?"

"Hop a freight headed for Vancouver. If we're going to starve we might as well do it in a warm climate."

"I don't know. Bert Wall did that. He was damned near dead when he got home. Said those railroad bulls are buggers. They club people!"

"They got to catch you first. What do you suggest, then?"

"Nothing. You got any dough?"

"No. But I think Tom would stake me to a little, just to get me out of the house. You have any?"

"Twenty bucks. Been saving it for a long time. I carry it slid inside my belt. Slit the stitches at the end and slid the bill inside, then sewed it up again."

"Good idea. If we have a little money, we won't have to panhandle. I don't think I could do that. One of those fat bastards turned me down, I'd want to kill him."

And so they decided to leave home. Alvin did not tell Martha, because he knew she would worry herself to death. Instead, he told her he was taking the bus to Harman, where he would stay with Hugh a few days and look for farm work.

Early in the morning they walked the four miles to the junction south of town where the freights stopped to take on water. They were in high spirits, two boys starting out on a great adventure.

"I've always wanted to see the mountains," Alvin said. "I've read about them."

"You've read about everything."

"Great chunks of granite with snow on top. Not all granite, though, strangely enough. There's one place at Frank, Alberta, where the whole side of a mountain slid off and buried part of the town."

"With people. . . ?"

"Yep. I read that they're still there."

When they reached the freight yards, filled with boxcars and switching tracks, Timmy asked, "Where do we catch this here-now freight?"

"Damned if I know. Let's ask that guy over there." They went up to a big man in a cap and Alvin said, "Excuse me, sir. Where do we catch the freight to Vancouver?"

The big man looked at him in disbelief. "You get the hell off railroad property or I'll run you in!" He grabbed Alvin by the arm.

"Let's go!" Timmy shouted, and started to run.

"Come back here, you little bastard," the big man shouted. He let go of Alvin and started after Timmy.

The boys dodged between two boxcars and ran down the side of a long line of cars.

"In here!" a voice shouted from one of the cars, and a hand reached down to Timmy, who scrambled up into the car with Alvin following.

The man inside slid the door shut, leaving a narrow slit through which he watched the big man lumber past.

"One thing about railway bulls, they don't run very fast."

"A policeman?"

"Yeah. And a mean bastard."

The man who had helped them was about thirty years old, very lean, and partly bald. He wore a week's growth of beard and smelled bad. When he opened his mouth the boys noticed that about four of his front teeth were missing.

"And we asked him which freight to catch for Vancouver!"

The lean one looked at them cannily. "You boys are really green. First time?"

"Yep."

"Could'a bin yer last. I've seen that bull break a man's arm just like nothing. What's yer names?"

"I'm Timmy and this is Alvin."

"Glad to meet ya. I'm Slim. Got any grub?"

The boys shared their sandwiches with him; he wolfed his share down in one bite.

"You kids stick with me," he said through a mouth jammed full of Martha's homemade bread. "Got any cash?"

Timmy started to answer, but Alvin interrupted. "No. Well, only a couple of bucks." He could see that Slim didn't believe him.

A steam-locomotive whistle sounded in the distance.

"There she comes," Slim said. "What we do is go to the end of the yard and just as she's picking up speed we hop aboard. That way we miss the bull, who will be clearing the riders off when it stops. We do that at every stop. Hop off at the edge of town when she's slowing down and hop on again at the other edge of town when she's picking up speed. Best place is about the middle of the train. We climb up to the top and try to find an empty car."

"What if there isn't one?"

"We ride on top, or on the ladder between the cars. You boys follow me and do what I do. Come on."

There proved to be nothing romantic or fun about riding freights. Nobody played the mouth organ or sang. It was windy, often cold, sometimes blazing hot, sometimes wet, and always dangerous.

The other riders were a mixture of old hands and first timers. Some had been riding back and forth across the country since the Depression began. There would be a rumour that Ford was taking on workers in Windsor and they would go there, only to find locked gates and NO MEN WANTED signs. Another rumour would take them to Halifax, another to Timmins for gold mining, another to Flin Flon. Usually they tried to spend the winter in Vancouver or Victoria. But wherever they went there were no jobs.

Being alert and active, Timmy and Alvin quickly caught on to the tricks of jumping on and off freights and dodging railroad police and Mounties. If they had to remain overnight in a town, they usually ended up in a jail cell in the town hall, where women volunteers would often provide a meal.

And with every jolting mile Alvin's hatred of the system grew. Many of the riders talked endlessly about ways to beat the system, but few were interested in changing it. So Alvin mostly kept his own counsel. He wrote verses and paragraphs in a notebook he carried. And he wrote a long letter to Martha, the only really close friend he had in the world except for Timmy.

Then, one bright clear May morning when they jumped off the freight on the outskirts of Calgary, they saw the mountains. They appeared to be about ten miles away, a line of jagged grey towers capped with snow.

"Look at that. Just look at that!" Alvin gasped. "The Rocky Mountains."

"Jesus," Timmy breathed. "Imagine!"

Alvin did a little dance there beside the railway track and chanted, "The Rockies, the Rockies, the great and wonderful mountains, the Rockies, the Rockies."

"Cheese it!" Timmy shouted. "The bulls!"

But he was too late. A railway cop was on them, swinging a pick handle and calling them every kind of bum and vagrant and useless bastard, any curse he could lay his tongue to. But the boys were too quick for him. Outside of a glancing blow on the rump, they escaped scot-free and tore down the side of the track, dodged between the cars, and left the policeman far behind.

Then they walked into Calgary.

"Kee-rist!" Timmy said as they neared the outskirts. "I'm so hungry my stomach thinks my throat's cut."

"Me, too."

"Let's ask at one of these houses."

"You mean beg?"

"Maybe we can offer to clean up the yard or wash the dog or something." Timmy held his stomach. "I've got to get something to eat."

"Which house?"

"That one there, the white one. Looks as though a kind person lives there."

"I've heard it's better to go to the back door."

So they opened the gate and went down a walkway beside the house and up to a neat back yard with a garden. Alvin stood looking at the back door and the window beside it. There was a potted geranium on the windowsill, and suddenly he was terribly homesick for Martha. He knocked on the door.

There was no answer.

"Let's go," he said.

"No, there's somebody in there. I can hear them." Timmy knocked again.

"Just a minute," called a voice from inside, and then

the door opened. A woman who looked to be in her mid-forties stood in the doorway with her purse in her hand. "Oh," she said. "I thought you were the milkman." But she didn't close the door.

"We hate to bother you like this, ma'am," Timmy said, "but we were wondering if we could clean up your yard or split some wood or something."

"No, I don't think so," the woman said. She was a short woman with black hair, neat, and rather plump.

"Sorry," Alvin muttered. Feeling ashamed and angry, he turned to go.

But Timmy couldn't. "We're awful hungry, ma'am."

The woman stared at the two pathetic figures. Dirty, matted hair, worn shoes. Her eyes softened.

"I think I could spare something. Wait here."

She turned and left, closing the door.

Timmy sat down on the stoop.

"She's not coming back," Alvin said. "Probably phoning the cops. Let's go."

"I can't," Timmy said. "Can't walk another step. Honest to God I can't."

So, reluctantly, Alvin sat down beside him. In a short while the woman opened the door and handed them a plate of salmon sandwiches and two cups of water. "I'm sorry, but this is all I have," she said. "My husband's been out of work for five years."

"Thank you, ma'am," Timmy said, and then on impulse added, "God bless you, for in as much as ye have done it unto the least of these. . . ."

The woman's eyes filled with tears. "I think I have some cookies, too." She closed the door.

"What the hell was that all about?" Alvin asked as they munched the sandwiches.

"I don't know," Timmy mused. "It just popped out. My ma chased me off to Sunday school every week. I guess it finally was good for something."

There and then Timmy discovered that he was a pretty good con man. He was the spokesman and the back doors of Calgary were his beat. At each door he had a new and better story. He was an orphan or had been driven from home by a cruel father or his mother was starving and there was nothing in the house for her to eat. Alvin was fascinated and a little ashamed to be part of it. Many doors were slammed in their faces, but others weren't; by the end of the week they were full of food and good spirits.

They applied for a few jobs and were kicked out of a few offices. "What I can't understand," Alvin said, "is why they are so damned miserable about it. You'd think we were asking for charity or something. All we want is a chance to work."

"Didn't help much when you told that last guy you were a supporter of Bible Bill."

"Yeah, I guess only the unemployed and farmers voted for him. I could sure use that twenty-five bucks a month he was talking about on the radio. Anyway, there's nothing here. Let's hop a freight and get into those mountains."

They spent the night in a coal shed and the next morning managed to get on a freight going west. They rode on one of the little platforms that ran along the roofs of the cars, swaying back and forth as the train went around curves and over trestles. And then, suddenly, they were in a tunnel. Smoke and hot cinders from the engine hit them like a blast from hell, blinding them and almost knocking them off the boxcar.

"Lie down!" Alvin gasped. "Quick!"

They got flat on their bellies, gripping the sides of the little platform, eyes closed, trying not to breathe. And just when they thought they could hang on no longer, they emerged into the sunlight again under the shadow of a majestic mountain.

At the next stop they got off the car near a stream, where they washed the soot from their faces and out of their eyes.

When the train was pulling out they saw an open boxcar door and managed to scramble into it. Inside there were two men who looked to be about thirty years old. They grasped the boys' hands and helped them into the car.

"Where you kids going?" the biggest man asked, with a smile Alvin didn't like at all.

"Vancouver," Timmy told him.

The big man put his hand on Alvin's shoulder.

"Us, too," he said. "You kids stick with us and we'll help you out. And maybe you can do something for us." His eyes were shining and his lips drew back in a leer.

"Thanks," Alvin said, and began to move away from him. But suddenly he was grasped around the waist, his arms pinned to his sides, and the other man was pulling at his trousers.

"Hey, cut that out!" Timmy yelled, and grabbed at Alvin's assailant. But the other man hit him a blow with his fist on the side of the head and knocked him down.

"Hold the little bugger," he shouted to the man behind Alvin. "Bend him over."

I'm being raped! Alvin thought. He kicked backwards and caught the man behind him on the shin with the heel of his boot. At the same time Timmy got to his feet and aimed a vicious kick at the crotch of the other man. He grunted and bent over and Timmy rushed him and shoved him out the open door. They heard his agonized cry as he hit the steep bank of the track and tumbled down.

Then both boys turned their attention to the other man.

"Okay, okay," he gasped. "Can't you take a little fun?"

At Banff the boys got off the train to see the town.

"After all," Timmy said, "this is one of the most famous playgrounds for the rich in the world. Do you know that Bing Crosby comes here to play golf?"

"Boo, boo, boo," Alvin crooned. "Now ain't that something?"

The young people they saw on the street were classy and obviously rich.

"Look at those bastards," Alvin said. "Don't know a thing about the Depression. Hell, their dads are probably making money out of it. I hate them."

But just the same, he envied them.

"You know," Timmy said, "I think we should clean ourselves up. A safety razor would only cost us a few cents and we could use the public washrooms in the park."

"What for?"

"Well, we might get a job. Maybe caddying or something."

So they did. Got a razor and shaved, washed their shirts and underwear, did what they could with their pants and windbreakers. They didn't look bad, but the air of poverty and destitution surrounded them like a blanket.

They walked through the Banff Springs Hotel, ignoring the looks of clerks and bellhops, and peeked into the dining room.

"You know, they throw out enough food in a day here to feed an average family for a week," Timmy said.

So they went around to the back of the hotel where the garbage cans were, but the garbage was in a wire enclosure with a lock on the gate.

"Now why in hell would they do that?" Alvin asked.

"Oh, I guess they'd have every bum in the country here if they didn't. The guests wouldn't like that."

"Guests! Parasites, you mean. Jesus, I'd like to get a gun and shoot them all."

"Let's get out of here," Timmy said uneasily, "and breathe some of that fresh mountain air."

"What about those jobs you mentioned?"

"Who we kidding? There won't be any jobs here. This place gives me the creeps."

They walked along the railroad tracks beside a mountain river, but their shoes had holes in the soles, and the gravel and cinders hurt their feet. When a freight came along and slowed for a steep grade they jumped on and rode on top of a car to the next stop, when they got inside again.

And so it went. At Revelstoke and Kamloops they managed to bum something to eat, which lasted them until they reached Vancouver.

They got off the train at the outskirts, avoided the cops, and walked downtown. The streets were full of unemployed people.

"Jeez, would you look at the big buildings," Timmy said. "This burg's even bigger than Calgary."

"Sure a lot different from Saskatoon,"Alvin agreed. "One thing about this trip, we're seeing some country. There's a big park in this city called Stanley Park. Let's see if we can find it."

"I'd like to see some ships," Timmy said. "I've never seen anything bigger than a motor-boat on Lake Manitou."

So they asked a passerby how to get to the park. Once there they watched freighters going under the Lions Gate Bridge into the harbour.

"Would you look at that one," Timmy said. "Must be a block long. I'd like to get a job on a ship like that and sail away from this country. Maybe to China or something."

"Me, too. I wonder how a guy could get a job like that. Maybe if we go down there to the dock we can ask somebody, or maybe stow away. I read about a kid who stowed away on a ship."

They found their way down to the docks, but the big metal gates were shut tight. They stood and watched a ship being unloaded.

"Bananas," Timmy said. "That whole ship's full of bananas."

Suddenly the clouds that were hanging low over the city opened up into a downpour. In no time the boys were soaking wet.

"Let's get the hell out of here," Timmy said. "I've seen enough of this place."

They went back to the centre of the city, soaking wet and uncomfortable. They found their way to a soup kitchen where, after standing in line in the rain for almost an hour, they were each handed a tin plate containing some beans and a piece of bread.

The rain kept coming, so they headed back to the freight yards and hopped a train going east.

"This is no life for man or beast," Timmy said. "I'm for home."

The ride east through the mountains was a repetition

of the ride west, but now they were experienced and did not get caught in any tunnels. Besides, they were heading home. The thought of warm baths and comfortable beds with sheets and enough to eat obsessed them. At least there was no more rain, but the heat of the day was oppressive.

When they got to the prairies the desolation was worse than it had been when they left. The wind blew constantly and was full of dust. They watched, fascinated, as the great dust clouds rolled across the fields where nothing could grow.

At the town of Medicine Hat they tried to scrounge a meal, but had no luck. They bought a can of sardines with their last fifteen cents.

"You know," Timmy said, as they sat on a park bench sharing the sardines, "I've got an uncle farms somewhere north of here."

"A rich uncle?"

"Search me. But if we went there I bet we could scrounge something to eat. Always something to eat on a farm."

"Yeah, that's true. How far is it?"

"I'm not sure. All my mother ever said was 'somewhere north of Medicine Hat.' "

"Well, let's hit the highway north. Do you know his name?"

"Same as Ma's - Greenway. We can ask. Somebody must know him."

They started out along the gravel highway going north. The few cars that passed them sent up clouds of dust that almost choked them. They tried hitching a ride, but with no luck.

When they had gone about two miles, Timmy gasped, "I gotta rest. Let's sit down for a while."

They went across a ditch and sat on the edge of a wheat field. The wheat was stunted and sparse. There was a big fat grasshopper on almost every stalk.

"You look kind of white," Alvin said to his friend. "How do you feel?"

"Not so hot." He bent over and vomited into the ditch.

"Hey, what gives?" Alvin asked, frightened. Ever since they had left he'd lived in fear of one of them getting sick.

"I don't know," Timmy said. "Got this pain in my gut." He groaned and held his side.

"How long you had that?"

"Just since this morning. Maybe it was the sardines."

"I ate 'em, too. Where does it hurt?"

"All over my gut. Kind of burning. Kind of comes and goes."

"Best thing we can do is get to your uncle's place fast. Come on." He helped Timmy to his feet and they climbed back to the side of the road.

They were in luck. A farmer driving a scruffy, underfed team of horses pulling a Bennett buggy was approaching. Alvin held up his thumb. The rig stopped.

"Hop aboard," the lean farmer said. "Not fast, but steady."

"Gosh, thanks," Alvin said and helped Timmy onto the wagon. "Do you know where Mr. Greenway lives?" he asked.

"He's my uncle," Timmy said.

"Greenway. Joe Greenway. Sure. Lives couple of miles east of here. You take the next side-road and just keep going till you come to it."

"Good. Thanks a lot."

They got off the Bennett buggy at the next side-road and started down a dusty dirt trail with desolate wheat fields on either side. They could see farm buildings in the distance.

"Think you can make it?" Alvin asked.

"Got to," Timmy gasped. "Not hurting so much now."

"Probably go away," Alvin reassured him, and silently prayed that it would. He was more frightened than he'd been since they'd left home. But as they approached the farm buildings he began to get a funny feeling. They looked desolate. The fences along both sides of the trail were piled with Russian thistle, that great, bushy tumbleweed that grew in profusion when nothing else would. There was no sign that anything had been driven along the road for weeks.

When they reached the farm driveway the sense of desolation grew. The yard was full of drifted sand that obliterated the driveway, and there was sand on the porch. Alvin saw that the front door of the house was banging loose in the wind. They entered the house, and the floor was covered with dust.

They stood in the doorway and stared. The furniture was still there, half buried in dust. And when they walked into the kitchen there were dirty dishes on the table, dishes that had been dirty for weeks.

"There's nobody here!" Timmy gasped. "They've gone!" And then he cried out ridiculously, "Anybody home? Uncle Joe?"

But there was no answer.

"They've been gone some time," Alvin said. "Jeez, just picked up and left, house, furniture, everything. Left it to the mice and gophers!"

Timmy sank down on a dust-covered chair. "Uncle Joe was a good farmer. He was proud of this place."

"Son of a bitch. Son of a bitch. Lousy bank probably closed him out!" Alvin was looking in the kitchen cupboards. "Bare as a spanked baby's ass."

Through the back window they could see a fenced garden with a few spears of something sticking up through the sand. They went out and found some small, grubby carrots and some parsnips. They carried them over to the well and tried the pump. At first nothing came, but as Alvin worked the handle faster and faster there was the sound of suction and then water came. They took turns holding their heads under the spout, then washed the carrots and ate them.

A lone chicken walked across the farmyard and went through the open barn door. They followed it and in a manger discovered a nest of eggs. Timmy was bending over gathering some chips of wood when he suddenly doubled over in pain and vomited up pieces of carrot and phlegm. He sank to the ground, moaning.

"Are you all right?" Alvin asked, realizing his question was foolish. "Come on," he said, putting his hand under Timmy's arm. "I saw a couch in the living room. You can lie on that."

He helped Timmy up the back steps and into the living room, where he collapsed on the couch, gasping and moaning. Alvin felt his forehead.

"Jeez, man, you're burning up!"

Alvin knew about appendicitis. A neighbour, aged twelve, had died from it, right in Saskatoon. It was a local tragedy, told and retold, how fast it had happened and how, after the appendix ruptured, there was no chance.

A doctor. He had to get a doctor. He ran into the hallway where he'd seen a phone on the wall, frantically turned the crank, and listened.

"Answer, damn you, answer," he breathed into the mouthpiece. But no one answered. The phone was dead.

When he got back to the living room Timmy had stopped groaning.

"It's kind of stopped. The pain. It's not so bad. But I can't get up."

Alvin looked at his friend's pasty grey face. The fever was raging inside him. He unlaced Timmy's tattered oxfords and pulled them off. Removed the holey, stinking socks. Even Timmy's feet were burning up. He ran upstairs and founds beds, but no covers or pillows. Two of the mattresses were gone, probably taken by the family, Alvin thought, when they left.

When he came down Timmy was delirious, talking meaningless gibberish. He seemed to be pleading with someone not to do something, and he was crying, "I didn't mean to, I didn't mean to!"

The sun was sinking over the flat, wasted land. A great flaming red ball. The wind had gone down, but the air was still full of dust. Alvin decided to light a fire in the kitchen range. Perhaps the smoke would attract a curious neighbour.

He found an old copy of *Western Producer*. The headline read, THIRTY-SEVEN DRIEST IN HISTORY. TOTAL CROP FAILURE PREDICTED. Probably the last thing Joe Greenway had read before leaving. Alvin built a fire and lit it, found a battered saucepan in a cupboard, and put some water on to boil. Then he put two of the eggs in the water. It was getting dark. He found a sooty barn lantern with a little kerosene left in it on the porch. He lit this and went back to Timmy.

Alvin had never seen death, but he knew he was soon to see it. Timmy's abdomen was terribly swollen: full, Alvin knew, of rotten poison. Peritonitis. He remembered the word from their hygiene classes in grade ten. There was no drug that could affect it. He knew Timmy's white corpuscles were fighting against the infection, but he knew they would lose.

He went outside and looked down the road, but no wagon was in sight. Nor could he see a light anywhere. Far off a coyote howled and a horned owl hooted from the direction of the barn. Maybe he should start walking back to town. But he couldn't leave Timmy alone. Besides, he knew that it was already too late.

He heard a scream from the house and ran inside. Timmy had tried to get up and was sprawled on the floor. Alvin heaved him back onto the couch, where he yelled again and fell unconscious.

Alvin went into the kitchen. The fire had burned itself out, but he figured the eggs were cooked. He fished them out of the water, broke the shell of one, and peeled it. Hard-boiled. It wasn't bad. The old hen must have just begun her set. He went back into the living room and lay down on the floor beside the couch. Timmy was still unconscious.

When he awoke it was getting light in the house and he realized he'd slept for hours. It was Timmy who wakened him, calling his name.

"Alvin, Alvin, I had the damnedest dream."

Alvin got up. Even in the dim light he could tell Timmy was dying.

"What kind of a dream?" he asked.

"I was home and my mother was there and my brother and sister and Dad and everybody. It was Christmas." His voice was barely a whisper and Alvin bent over to hear what he was saying. "God, it was clear, Al. I could see them all. Dad had on that old green sweater with the hole in the elbow." He sighed. "But I wasn't there, Al, I wasn't there. They kept asking, 'Where is Timmy? He should be here.' "

"Yeah. Dreams are crazy."

"Don't leave me, Al. Please. No use going for help now."

"This damned place! Nobody's been up this road since we came. They must have all gone north looking for better land."

"Could you get me some cold water? I'm burning up."

Alvin went out to the pump and looked in every direction for a sign of life. A flickertail stuck its head out a hole and chirped at him. High in the sky a hawk circled. There was no wind. The look and feel of that silent, still dust-hazy day would remain in Alvin's mind for as long as he lived.

When he got back with the water, Timmy had lapsed into unconsciousness and he never woke up. Alvin was never exactly sure when Timmy died. He just stopped breathing and lay with a stupid grin on his face, as though he had thought of an outrageous pun.

And then there was a sound of snorting and rattling on the road and a ramshackle Model A pick-up ploughed through the drifted sand in the driveway. A young man of about Alvin's age leaned out the broken window on the driver's side.

"Saw the smoke. Wondered who was here."

Alvin had a crazy thought that Timmy would have quipped, "Nobody but us chickens." He led the young man into the living room.

"He's dead."

Together they loaded Timmy on the back of the pick-up and covered him with some binder canvas and hauled him off to Medicine Hat. They left him with a hardware merchant who doubled as an undertaker, and Alvin phoned Timmy's home.

When Mr. McCall answered the phone, Alvin told him what had happened. There was a long silence, and then a tired voice said, "Well, you'd better get a coffin there and have it loaded on the express car of the next train. Send it COD. I'll find the money somewhere to pay the charges."

And that was the end of Timmy. Nineteen years old and never been kissed.

Alvin caught a freight that took him all the way to Regina and then another home. He never went on the bum again.

Chapter Eleven

Hugh hadn't wanted to teach school, hadn't wanted to live in Saskatchewan, hadn't wanted to be poor.

"The trouble with members of your own family," he said, "is that they think they have the right to ask questions nobody else would ask."

It was Olive who had asked the question. No beating around the bush, no subterfuge, just, "Why in hell did you never get married, Hugh?"

"What?"

"Come on. You can tell us. It's truth time. We're all too old for it to make any difference. I know you're not a pansy."

"How would you know that, now?"

"Oh, sisters have a way of knowing things."

"Hmmm. Well, there are all sorts of gradations of pansyism, my dear. I know homosexuals who are married and have children."

"Were married."

"Well, yes."

"Anyway we can rule that out. Why did you never get married?"

"Well, since you were kind enough to ask, sister dear, I'll give you a straight answer. I never found a woman I wanted to live with."

Tom laughed. "Hell, brother, no man wants to live with a woman, not really, but the thing is that a wife, well, she's got something he can't get anywhere else without a lot of expense and trouble."

"You mean it combines the 'maximum of temptation with the maximum of opportunity,' " Gwen said.

"So now we have another marriage expert talking," Olive said, and then, noting the look on her sister's face, added, "I'm sorry, I didn't mean that."

"I was merely quoting," Gwen said.

Tom stepped in to prevent a delicate situation from becoming troublesome. "Getting back to you, Hugh. I seem to remember you being all hot and bothered over a little farm girl out there at Harman."

"Well, brother, I see you've lost none of your tact and *savoir-faire*," Hugh replied.

"You got me, brother." Tom laughed. "Soon as you start using them big words, I'm finished."

The conversation went on to other things, but Hugh wasn't listening. Why hadn't he got married? And what would his life have been like with Elaine? Wonderful, that's what it would have been like. In one way, he knew that. But what about other ways? And what about Elaine? He knew he had to find out, to settle it once and for all in his mind. It was time, time to take that trip to Harman.

Harman, Saskatchewan, was the town to which Hugh went to teach in 1934.

He had distinguished himself at normal school, as he had in high school. Not because he wanted to be there, but because whatever he did he did conscientiously and well. After graduation he almost abandoned the idea of teaching, for there was an abundance of teachers, partly because there was no one leaving the profession, as had happened when teaching was considered a stepping-stone to other professions, and partly because more people than usual attended the provincial normal schools. More than half his classmates never did find teaching jobs. But with the perversity that fate often indulges in, he got a break. Will told him about an old friend he'd happened to meet downtown, a man named Alec Roarie, who was chairman of the Harman school board.

"We're looking for a principal for our continuation school," Alec told him.

"Look no further. My son Hugh just graduated from normal school with high honours."

"No experience?"

"None. But he's a very bright lad."

"Hmm . . . Well, we had an experienced teacher with a B.A. degree and he got us into more damned trouble. Couldn't keep his hands off the senior girls. Knocked one of them up. Damned shame. Trouble is, we can't pay enough to get a really good experienced teacher. Maybe a young feller who's full of ambition would fill the bill. Where is he now?"

"At home. Why don't you come up and meet him? Martha'd be delighted to see you."

"Still live in the same place?"

"Oh, no. Lost that house, along with everything else. But I can still manage a wee dram for you."

And that was the way it went. Alec, who owned a general store in Harman, dreaded advertising the position and ploughing through the hundreds of applications they would get. So he agreed to talk to Hugh.

Although he had no more than a grade-eight education (more than either of the two farmers who were also on the school board), Alec tried to do what was right. He went over Hugh's scholastic records, noting the prizes he had won, and was impressed with his writing for the school paper and his work with the dramatic society.

"We need a young man with ideas and spunk and go-gettingness. Better come out and meet the rest of the board."

And so it came about that Hugh took the train to Harman and met with the other members of the board. Harman, he discovered, was a miserable little town consisting of three grain elevators, a lumber yard, a general store, a Chinese café, a town hall with a pool-room in the front, a telephone office, a run-down hotel, a garage, two churches, and about a dozen houses.

The three-room school, which drew most of its pupils from the surrounding farms, taught the full elementary course. A primary room with grades one to four, an intermediate room with grades five to eight, and a senior room with grades nine, ten, eleven, and twelve. For taking charge of this school and its sixty-eight students and teaching all the subjects in the senior room, the board was willing to pay Hugh nine hundred dollars a year.

"It's a danged sight more than I made last year," said board member Bert Wiley, who farmed two sections just out of town.

Anton Friesen, the other board member, who farmed in the other direction from town, laughed hollowly. "Yeah, last year I shipped ten steers to Winnipeg and got a bill for the freight!"

The school was an embarrassment to these men. According to the law, they had to keep it open, but the tax revenue was so small from the dried-out farmers of the district that it was well-nigh impossible.

Hugh eyed the board members with distaste and disgust. He had to be nice to these men. Had to persuade them to hire him. They knew nothing about education and cared less. Couldn't even speak decent English. But because they were members of the board, they were in a position of power; they could make or break him. If he missed this school, his chances of getting another were slim. The province was full of unemployed teachers, and many who were employed were teaching for their room and board. He couldn't go home and face Tom, who practically supported the family. And he couldn't go on the bum. He had to have this job.

And so he became a salesman, using every trick he could think of to persuade these men. He outlined all his accomplishments and invented a few more. Finally, as the sun was going down over the dusty prairie, they came to their decision. He could have the job. He found out later that they'd been paying the horny principal twelve hundred a year.

The two months of summer holidays were the worst he could remember. He still had his paper route; the rest of the time he helped make and deliver marmalade. And he carted books home from the public library for night reading. He developed a distaste for his family that he never wholly got over.

On the first day of September, a Saturday, Tom drove him to Harman with all his worldly goods piled into the rumble seat of the Buick. When Tom saw Harman he exploded. "Jesus Christ, brother, what a dump! How many people live here?"

"Seventy-one, at the latest count."

"Where you going to live?"

"That green house over there. Frank Walper, the garage man, and his wife. They're going to board me."

"Bored is right. What do they do for excitement in this burg?"

"Don't know. I'll be too busy for much excitement."

"Never too busy, brother, for a little yum-yum – and you never know where you're going to find it. Watch out for the farmers' daughters."

They stopped in front of the Walpers' house, a one-and-a-half-storey structure with a neat yard, a caragana hedge around the property, and a large garden. Hugh knocked on the door and a pretty, petite woman with dark hair, cropped close to her head, answered it. She reminded him of Colleen Moore.

"Oh," she said, smiling broadly. "You must be Mr. Windmar. I've been expecting you. I'm Jenny Walper."

Hugh introduced himself and Tom.

"Well," Tom said easily. "Just goes to show you can't judge the contents of a town by its outside looks."

Jenny Walper laughed easily, a trifle coquettishly, Hugh thought.

Tom helped him with his trunk and boxes of books, which they took to a small room upstairs under the eaves. It was neat and tidy, with frilled curtains and a crotcheted cover on the washstand.

"Not big," Mrs. Walper said, "but warm. The stovepipe from the living room sees to that."

"It's fine, thanks," Hugh said. "I think before I unpack

I'd like to go over to the school." What he really wanted was to get Tom out of there before they would have to ask him to stay for supper.

So they went to the school, on the opposite side of town beside the highway, and inspected the rooms. It was T-shaped, with a central hall, one room on each side, and the senior room at the end. Across the hall from the senior room was a small principal's office.

They looked into the intermediate room. Tom sat down in one of the larger desks at the back. "This is about my speed. First time I've been in a school since they kicked me out."

"Go on. They never kicked you out."

"No, I went on my own accord. And damned glad to do it." He looked up at the blackboard; the letters of the alphabet were printed along the top.

"Jesus Murphy, schools have changed since I went. I remember one teacher I had. Boy, oh boy, was she stacked. I used to ask her to help me with arithmetic because then she bent over my desk – "

"Cut it out, Tom. There may be somebody around."

"Pardon me, brother, I forgot." He got up and looked in the other rooms. They were empty. Hugh wished he would go. Tom made him uneasy.

"That's quite a little landlady you got there, brother," he said. "I'd watch out for her. Had a girl friend looked just like her. Screwed like a mink."

"Oh, for God's sake. You've got a mind like a sewer!"

"Shit's my name, but they call me Shite for short." Tom laughed loudly. "Just the same, be careful. Don't get yourself shot by an irate garage man."

"I'll be careful."

Tom stood up. "What say we go over to the Chink's and get some food. I'm starved."

"Good idea."

They went back to the main street and into the Chinese restaurant, which had a counter on one side and four booths on the other. A man sitting at the counter looked them over. Hugh realized that from now on everything he did in this town would be noted and reported.

Tom nodded to the man. "Hi. Hotter'n a fiddler's fart, eh?"

The man guffawed. "Sure is."

As they sat in one of the booths, Hugh whispered, "Cut it out. I've got to live in this town!"

"Well, pardon me for living." Tom produced a flask from his pocket and poured from it into one of the glasses on the table. "Snort?"

"No! What the hell are you trying to do?"

"Sorry." Tom drank his drink. "Nobody saw that little gesture."

A short, fat Chinese man with a big smile appeared at the booth and handed each a slip of paper on which a menu was hand-printed. Bacon and eggs. Liver and onions. Salisbury steak and peas.

"Me Pop," the man said. "Welcome to Harman."

"Thanks, Pop," Tom said. "This is your new teacher."

"Oh, new teacher. Velly nice, velly nice. You whack them kids, eh?" He laughed loudly.

"You damn betcha," Tom said. "This is one tough hombre. Pass the word."

The Chinese man left, still laughing.

"For God's sake, will you stop it, Tom!" Hugh hissed. "You don't realize what this kind of town is like."

The meal turned out to be very good. After they ate, Tom pressed Hugh's hand and said seriously, "Goodbye, brother. Good luck. A word of advice: never admit you don't know anything. Fake it. None of these yokels know the difference." Then he grinned. "Don't do anything I wouldn't do." He stepped off the curb and got into his car, waved once, and drove off.

Standing on the broken sidewalk in front of the restaurant, watching the Buick go down the dusty street, it was all Hugh could do to stop from calling his brother back. He felt a hollow in the pit of his stomach. Alone!

He walked down to the end of the street and out across

the prairie towards what looked like a baseball backstop. The dry grass crackled under his oxfords and swarms of grasshoppers flew up in front of him.

Then he went back to the school and let himself in. Tomorrow there would be sixty-eight kids in the building. All under his charge. Fifteen of them, in four different grades, in his room. And he had to teach them everything: math, English, trigonometry, history, French, Latin, physics, chemistry. How was it possible? He pulled open the centre drawer of the desk and took out the register. Read the names. Five in grade nine, six in grade ten, three in grade eleven, and one in grade twelve. Elaine Sanderson. He wondered if a farm girl could stay in school long enough to get her senior matric. Well, she'd just have to take her chances.

"Hello there," a female voice said from the doorway.

Hugh stood up and mumbled a greeting.

"I'm Jean McTavish, the intermediate teacher." She came forward and held out her hand. Hugh took it.

"Hugh Windmar."

She appeared to be about twenty-five years old. Brown hair, large, intelligent eyes, good figure, and a way of walking and standing that impressed Hugh.

"Getting ready for tomorrow?"

"God." Hugh waved his hand at the register. "How is it possible?"

She looked at him, her big eyes showing surprise. "Is this your first teaching job?"

"Yeah. Green as grass. All these subjects. . . ."

"A little tip – do the best you can and don't worry about what you can't do. These kids are marvellous at working by themselves."

"They'll have to be." Then he remembered that he was the principal. He tried to remember how a principal acts. Straighten up, he told himself. Maintain the proper distance between you and your staff. "Yes, yes, to be sure."

The intelligent face changed ever so slightly. "Would you like to exchange any classes with me? Mr. Ramsey had me take the senior English. He was a math and science specialist."

"Uh . . . thank you, but I think not. Not just at first, anyway."

She was about to leave when another woman entered the room. This one was older, thin-faced, with a set smile. She, too, held out her hand.

"Miss Anderson!"

"How do you do. I take it you are the primary teacher."

"Yes, I have been for six years now. Some of my earlier pupils are already in your room."

"I see. I'm Hugh Windmar. I trust everything is in readiness for tomorrow?"

Jean McTavish looked as though she were going to laugh, but stopped herself. "Oh, yes. Ready for the thundering herd."

Hugh assured them he would see them both in the morning and then left. As he approached the Walper house he noticed a tall, rangy man in overalls and a cloth cap clipping the hedge. The man put the clippers down when he saw Hugh and came towards him, holding out an immense paw. His lean, craggy face wrinkled into a grin.

"Welcome, teacher. I'm Frank Walper." He led the way into the house. "Wow, haven't seen this place look so spic-and-span since Christmas."

It was, Hugh soon came to realize, Frank's way of showing affection, or something, for his wife. To kid her about everything. Housework, cooking, even the condition of his clothes. Hugh could sense that she didn't like it.

Now she blushed and said, "I meant to ask you and your brother to come back for lunch."

"Uh, we ate at the Chinaman's."

"Old Pop's swill?" Frank laughed. "Get out the stomach pump."

"Actually, it wasn't bad."

"Must have been one of his better days. Well, you won't get much better here." He laughed again. Frank had a habit of laughing at every dig he made at his wife, Hugh noticed, as though that somehow made it all a joke. Jenny never laughed, just looked pained and embarrassed.

"Aren't you going to put something on besides those old overalls for supper?" she asked.

"Why?"

"Well, because it's Sunday, for one thing."

"Okay. But I can't afford fancy duds like the teacher here." Frank laughed again. Hugh was dressed in his only good suit, carefully brushed and pressed, and a clean white shirt. He was always neat and tidy in his attire, regardless of how hard up he might be.

The Walper children came in from Sunday school. Two boys, six and eight, dressed in their Sunday best. Jenny introduced them: Percy and Herbert. Hugh greeted them in what he considered to be the proper school-principal manner.

"Ma says you are going to live with us," Percy, age six, said.

"And that means we'll have to sleep in the room in the cellar again," his brother added.

"Not the cellar," Jenny corrected, "the basement. Actually it's a very nice room. Run along now and get washed for supper."

"Nice children," Hugh said. He could see that their mother was very proud of them.

"Yeah, they're okay," Frank said. "Would you like a beer?"

"Frank! Really!" This from Jenny.

So here it was. Teachers didn't drink. Alec had made a big point of that at the interview. Everybody in the district older than sixteen, and some younger, drank like fish. But not the teacher. Supposed to set a good example.

"No, thanks," Hugh said, and then added hopefully, "not just now." He wanted Frank to like him, wanted to be a member of this family. But he could tell there were going to be troubles.

The dinner was very good. Roast beef with Yorkshire pudding, mashed potatoes, and creamed carrots, with lemon pie for dessert. Frank commented on every item, making out that they never ate this well except when there was company.

Hugh kept changing the subject. "Is the CCF very active here?" he asked.

"That bunch of socialists!" Frank exploded. "Oh, yeah, they're active. The preacher - our own United Church minister - is planning to be the candidate at the next election. A preacher!"

"What do you care?" his wife asked. "You never go to church."

"Nope - last time I was there they married me and I ain't never been back."

Hugh watched Jenny cringing at the reference to their wedding and at the word "ain't." Frank, Hugh came to realize, purposely used bad grammar to annoy his wife.

"Well, at least they're trying to do something about this Depression," Hugh ventured.

"What can they do? Make it rain? You know, we haven't had a decent rain in this district since twenty-nine. Take money from the rich and give it to the poor? Fat chance! I tell you - "

"Frank," his wife cut in, "Mr. Windmar could use some more meat, I'm sure."

"Sure, sure." He sliced off a big piece of meat and plopped it on Hugh's plate.

"Our Sunday school teacher said we should all help one another," Herbert said.

"What the hell does she know about anything?" Frank exploded. "That dried-up old maid."

"Miss Waslenski was perfectly right," Jenny said. "I'm sure your daddy thinks so, too." She gave Frank a look that clearly said he'd damned well better.

"Sure, sure."

"What's a dried-up old maid?" Percy asked.

"There's no such thing," Jenny said. "It's just your father's joke." The way she said the word "joke" indicated that it was anything but funny.

"An old maid is a woman who doesn't have a man or

kids of her own and tells other people's kids – "

"Frank!"

"I notice you have a radio," Hugh cut in. "Do you get Jack Benny?"

"Sure do, direct from Salt Lake City. How about that? Baseball games, too. You like baseball?"

"Yes. Rather."

"The World Series will soon be on. Should be good. Two good teams."

"Frank is a baseball pitcher," Jenny said with some pride. "Last year's Sports Day, he hired out with the Rosetown team and they won first prize. A hundred dollars."

"Each?" Hugh asked innocently.

Frank's laugh split the air. "Each? Jesus Murphy, no! The whole team. We had to split it nine ways. You play baseball?" he added hopefully.

"No, not really."

"Oh. Well, how about another piece of pie?"

"Well, just a small one. I'm pretty full, but I can't resist that pie. It's the best I've ever eaten."

Jenny blushed becomingly. "I thought the crust a little tough."

Frank guffawed again. "Did you ever see a woman admit that her pie crust was perfect? It's always 'a little tough.' " He raised his voice to a falsetto to imitate his wife.

Jenny got up from her chair and went into the living room, head held high.

"Don't go away mad," Frank laughed.

Hugh wanted to tell him to lay off. Couldn't he see that this nonsense could ruin their marriage? But he didn't. He bent over his pie and ate it slowly and deliberately.

Still seated, Frank leaned over, took a round can of Player's fine cut from the sideboard, and placed it on the table before him. Took a package of papers from the bib pocket of his overalls, blew one free, took a pinch of tobacco, and expertly rolled a cigarette. He pushed the can over to Hugh.

"Smoke?"

Another decision. Teachers weren't supposed to smoke.

The children had left the table, and Hugh had to have a smoke. He took a package of Turrets from his jacket pocket.

"Try one of these."

"Tailor-mades. Well, I guess." Frank put the rolled cigarette back in the top of the can and took one of Hugh's. "One thing you'll learn about women, if you ever get married. . . ." Frank drew in a big draught of smoke and sucked it down into his lungs. "They're mighty touchy."

Hugh bit his tongue again. Whatever he did, he wouldn't get into any of their arguments. Not in any way, ever.

From the living room came the theme of the Jack Benny show and they went in to listen and laugh. It was followed by the Eddie Cantor show and then the national news with Charles Jennings. There were strikes and riots and a statement from R.B. Bennett that any subversion would be squelched with an iron heel.

After the news Frank stretched elaborately and said, "Time to hit the hay." He got up, went into the kitchen, and got a drink of water from the pail on the sink, came back through the living room, and started up the stairs. "Coming?"

"Not just yet," Jenny said. "Think I'll read a while."

"Okay." He went on up the stairs, and Hugh realized that in that short exchange was great significance.

"What are you reading?" Hugh asked.

"Oh, just a silly romance." She held it up. "Passes the time."

"Do you like short stories?"

"Well, that depends. I like the short-short stories in *Liberty*."

"Have you read any of Hemingway's?"

"Who?"

"Ernest Hemingway, an American writer. *A Farewell to Arms*, *The Sun Also Rises*. . . ."

"Are those short stories?"

"No, novels. I have them with me, if you'd like to read them. But right now I'm reading his short stories."

"Why?"

"Well, as a matter of fact, I've been trying to write some short stories myself."

"That's very interesting." She pulled her feet up into the chair. "Have you sold any?"

"Well, one, to *Story Magazine*. I got twenty-five dollars."

"You'll never get rich that way."

Hugh frowned. "One of Hemingway's short stories is the best I've ever read. It's called 'The Short Happy Life of Francis Macomber.' Set in Africa."

"Africa? Oh, I'd love to go to Africa."

"Would you? This story is about a man named Macomber who is hunting big game in Africa with his wife. His wife is a bitch."

"Oh."

Hugh didn't know if Jenny's comment indicated shock or interest. "They're camped out on the Serengeti Plain and there is a white hunter with them."

"A what?"

"A guide. A man who is expert at hunting big game. They call them white hunters."

"What happens?"

"Well, Macomber meets this lion and runs away. The white hunter shoots it. And – well, the wife has an affair with the white hunter – at least, Macomber thinks she does – and later shoots her husband."

"How terrible. On purpose?"

"We don't know, exactly. Macomber, who is terribly upset because his wife despises him for being a coward, faces a water buffalo, which is more dangerous than a lion, and shoots it. But his wife is standing back a ways. She sees the buffalo running at her husband and shoots. She gets her husband in the back of the head. The question is, did she do it on purpose or was she trying to save him from the charging buffalo? It's a marvellous story, really. The whole business of husband and wife is summed up there."

Jenny sat musing. "I've never had an affair. If I did I'm afraid I'm the one who'd get shot."

"I'll lend you the book. I have quite a number of other books that you might like."

"Sexy ones?"

"Well, yes, some of them."

"Well, I must go to bed." She jumped up. "Be sure and turn off the Aladdin lamp before you come up or it will smoke terribly." She ran up the stairs to her husband.

Hugh thought that, since school started the next day, he'd better get a good night's sleep. He went up to his room, which was at the other end of a short hallway from the Walpers' room. As he opened his door he heard a giggle from the other room.

As he lay awake in the dark room, he could hear faint noises from across the hall. Bed-springs creaking, muffled laughter. In his mind he could see them in there on the bed, the tight, compact little body covered by the big, rangy one. He developed such a terrific erection he knew he'd never get to sleep without doing something about it. He did something about it.

At seven-thirty the next morning Jenny called him to breakfast. The dining-room table was set for two.

"Where's Mr. Walper?"

"Oh, he left an hour ago. Some of the farmers need repairs for their binders and they come in early."

"How was the crop around here?"

"Terrible. But there is some. Bacon and eggs?"

"No, thanks. Just an egg and some toast and coffee."

From the kitchen she called, "Did you sleep well on that bed?"

"Very well, thanks," he lied.

She came in with his breakfast. "So this is your first day. It's always the worst. Just don't let any of those big boys put anything over on you."

"Big boys?"

"The farm boys will all be working in the harvest, but there's Leonard Green, lives out near the Sandersons and never works. He's a terror. My goodness, he's bigger than you are. Elaine won't be there, either."

"Elaine?"

"Sanderson. She's in grade twelve. A lovely girl. It's a shame."

"What do you mean?"

"Well, she lives out on a big farm just south of town and she has eight brothers and sisters."

"Some family."

Jenny made a face. "Disgusting. That old Bob Sanderson worked his wife to death, and now he's trying to do the same to Elaine."

"You mean she's looking after the family?"

"She and John. He's the oldest son. Works like a dog on that farm. And such a nice boy. Boy – he's a man. Elaine cooks and sews and – well, she does everything a mother would do."

"Not everything, I hope."

She paused in pouring his coffee and looked down on him. "No, not that. At least I hope not." As she bent over, her left breast pressed ever so lightly against his shoulder. "Of course, the other girls help, and the boys. They all work like dogs on that farm. You'll have two other Sandersons in your room – Clifford is in grade eleven and Tim in grade nine."

Hugh was beginning to feel a little panic. He pushed back his chair. "I think that's all I can eat, thanks, Mrs. Walper. I want to get to school early."

Before he left Saskatoon, he'd been given some advice by an experienced teacher: "On the first day of a new job, be at school at eight o'clock. Everybody will be watching you and talking about you. Keep that up for a week or so and you'll establish the reputation of always getting to school early, being conscientious. After that they'll quit watching and talking, and you can arrive when you like. Same with discipline. Be tough as hell the first month and then you can gradually let up."

He went up to his room, put on his jacket, picked up

the books he wanted to take, and came down the stairs. Jenny was in the living room.

"All ready for the fray?" she said, and when he only nodded and went out the front door she called after him, "Good luck!"

Chapter Twelve

As Hugh Windmar drove Tom's Buick along the highway towards Harman, he was struck by the contrast between what he saw and the conditions he remembered from forty-six years earlier, when he had first travelled that road.

In the first place, instead of the gravel road that existed then, he was on a wide, paved highway. The farm buildings he passed were painted and prosperous-looking. They'd all have electricity, he realized. What a difference that would make. Off to the right he saw the buildings of a potash mine – the peculiar cone-shaped holding bins, the stacks of the refinery belching smoke – and a huge pile of sodium chloride, the residue of the refining process. Potash and oil and good crops and uranium, he thought, have made this depressed have-not province into one of the most prosperous in the land.

And as he drove he realized that the rhythm of a Tennyson poem was running through his head: "Elaine the fair, Elaine the lovable, Elaine the lily maid of Astolat." My God, but she was lovable, he thought. And, like the lily maid, slated for tragedy. He tried to think of other things.

Of that first day in school. Green as grass. Knowing practically nothing about teaching. Nineteen years old, barely older than the senior students. From paper-boy to principal in one year.

Of all the things that had happened to him since, hobnobbing with the great and near-great of the land, meeting the governor general to receive an award, victories and defeats, nothing stood out in his mind as much as that first day at school.

He had arrived early, to set a good example. Everything he did was supposed to set an example in the community. Don't drink, don't smoke, don't make love. Especially don't make love. Shortly after he got to the school that first morning, Jean McTavish came into his room and sat down on one of the desks in the front row. She looked at him quizzically as he sat frowning into a book on his desk.

"We don't usually do much on the first day," she said.

"Oh?"

"It's up to you, of course, but usually we register the kids, assign them to their seats, give them a list of textbooks, and let them go."

"Yes, that's what I intend to do."

It was obvious that she wanted to talk more, reassure him, but his still, official demeanour precluded that. She got up to go.

"Uh, Miss McTavish, could you spare a moment?"

"Yes, of course."

"I've been thinking of what you said about exchanging classes. I would like to teach grammar in your room. Would that be agreeable to you?"

"It sure would."

"Yes. Well, you see, I recall that many students in high school had difficulty with Latin grammar because they had a poor grounding in English grammar."

"And you think I might give them a poor grounding?" Her half-smile took away any sting from the remark.

"Not necessarily."

"Well, actually I loath teaching grammar, and I'm not really very good at it. I think switching is an excellent idea."

"Good."

"What can I teach in your room?"

"Well, now, that's a problem. What would you prefer?"

"Well, I specialized in French at university."

"University?"

"Yes, I have a B.A."

"Interesting." A B.A., and he had a lousy normal-school certificate. He felt afraid and incompetent. "Yes, I think it would be most satisfactory for you to take the French." French had been his only poor subject.

Later, when he got to know her and they became fast friends, she admitted that she thought him the damnedest stuffed shirt she'd ever seen.

"How did you put up with me?" he asked.

"Oh, I knew you'd change. At least I hoped so."

When the pupils came in and settled into their seats, looking up at him with a mixture of interest, hope, and defiance, he thought he'd better make a little speech.

"We are all here for the same reason. To learn. Not to have fun or play games, but to learn. And we have the same goals – to see that each one of you learns enough and retains enough to pass into the next grade. Anything that interferes with that goal will not be tolerated. There will be only one form of discipline here. Not the strap, or detention after school, but expulsion. Anyone who disrupts the smooth running of this classroom will be expelled. And he won't be admitted back until he brings one of his parents and we have an understanding."

A hand went up at the back, a boy about as tall as Hugh and considerably heftier.

"Yes?"

"What if it's a girl?"

A little titter from the class.

Never answer a question. Ask another. "Why do you ask that" – he looked down at the register – "Leonard, is it?"

"You said 'he.' What if it's a girl who dis... dis... What you said?"

"Have you any particular girl in mind?"

A louder titter. Unknowingly, Hugh had hit a delicate spot with Leonard. "I was using the rhetorical 'he.' " Hugh smiled. "In any case, I trust the situation will not arise. Now, on to other matters." He felt good; in any joust of wits he knew he could beat any of these yokels. He did the necessary things and dismissed the class for the day.

As they filed out, a girl approached his desk with a friendly smile on her face. It was the first time he'd noticed Elaine. She certainly wasn't the prettiest girl he'd ever seen, but she was far and away the most attractive. Never afterwards could he remember her exact appearance. It was the essence of her, the warmth, the kindness, the generosity, the downright lovableness of her, and, of course, her smile and self-assurance.

"I'm Elaine Sanderson," she said easily. "Your one and only grade-twelve student."

"Yes?"

"Well, I have this problem. It's harvest time and I have to stay home for a couple of weeks and help." Her smile said that this was the most natural and reasonable request in the world.

"Two weeks. That will put you behind."

"Oh, I know, but I'm used to it. Happens every year. So I work like a dog and catch up."

"Well, I don't know . . . perhaps I should talk to your father about this."

"Talk to Dad?" Her eyes were wide with surprise. "Fat lot of good that would do. He'd be delighted if I quit school altogether and just kept house. But I'm not going to."

"You want an education."

"I do, and I'm going to get it."

"Good for you. Well, I suppose if you must, you must. I'll help all I can."

"Thank you."

From the corner of his eye Hugh had seen big Leonard Green hovering near the door. When Elaine went out, Leonard joined her. From his window, Hugh could see them walking across the school yard together towards the bar
In a little while they emerged, bareback, on their ho
They galloped out through the gate and down th
together.

Later he asked Jean McTavish where Leonar

"On the farm next to the Sandersons. I think he's sweet on Elaine."

"Oh."

"At least as sweet as that big lout can be on anybody but himself."

"And Elaine?"

"Don't worry about her. She's got ambition, that girl. Not likely to marry a farmer. Unless of course. . . ."

"Yes?"

"Unless her biology betrays her. Elaine is a lively, lovely girl. Loaded with 'It.' "

"I see. Like Clara Bow."

"Exactly. And Leonard is handsome and persistent, and determined to get her into the hay."

"How do you know so much about her?"

"Well, if you must know, Elaine's brother John and I are engaged. Have been for two years." Her expression changed. "This damned Depression."

"May I walk you home?"

"You most certainly may."

As they walked towards her boarding house on the other side of town, he asked her, "I was curious as to why you'd stayed here so long, with your obvious ability and qualifications."

"But now you're not – curious, I mean. Love is a strange thing. If anybody had told me a few years ago that what I'd want most in life was to marry a farmer and raise his kids, well. . . ."

"If love does that, I shall try to avoid it."

"I have an idea you are not enamoured of the teaching profession."

"Hah. At nine hundred lousy dollars a year, with the work load I have?"

"Why did you take it?"

"What else? I'm not suited to riding freight trains."

"I see."

He kicked a huge, ripe pigweed plant and sent it flying. "So I shall work hard and see to it that these kids get the education they deserve. It's going to mean burning a lot of midnight oil, but next year will be easier – I hope."

"What do you really want to do?"

Normally he resented prying questions, but Jean was so open and fine that he wanted to be her friend. "Write. Got my eye on that *Liberty* short-short story that pays one thousand bucks. But it's going to have to wait."

"And then?"

"Then Toronto. When I've sold enough to establish some credentials, I shall shake the dust of this godforsaken province from my heels forever."

He said it with such vehemence and conviction that Jean stopped and looked at him. "I think you will. And there is only one thing that can stop you."

"I know. Falling in love with a luscious farmer's daughter. I shall avoid it."

"They'll be out to get you. Handsome young school principals are considered very good catches in this neck of the woods." They had reached her boarding house.

"Do you like to walk?" he asked her.

"Love it. About the only recreation there is here. Unfortunately, John works too hard for that old slave driver of a father to have much time or energy for walking."

"Then perhaps he wouldn't object if we became walking partners."

Her laugh was like music. "I'm sure he wouldn't."

"Next Sunday morning?"

"No, Sunday is John's only day off. I devote all of it to him. Besides, everybody in Harman goes to church. The entire Sanderson family arrives in that Oldsmobile of theirs, all clean and shining. Elaine sees to that."

"And you?"

"Oh, yes, indeed. I sing in the choir. So does John. Singing is one of the things we love to do together. Do you sing?"

"Like a crow. Can't even carry a tune."

"Not really."

"Yep. When I was in public school the teacher said, 'Now everybody sing out – but Hugh.' "

"How awful!"

Hugh took a little notebook from his pocket and made a notation: "Eight o'clock Saturday, walk with Jean."

"Not too early?" he said.

"Nope. My, you are organized."

"Got to be. Well, goodbye. I enjoyed our walk."

He went home and spent the rest of the day and evening making out his timetable and preparing his lessons for the next day. And that's the way it was every day and evening. Every minute he wasn't teaching, he was preparing lessons for the next day. He never left the school until six o'clock, working by the light of an Aladdin lamp. And he was always there at eight in the morning. He worked through recess and the noon hour.

Sometimes at night he would go for long walks under the canopy of stars. The wind invariably went down with the sun, and night was the best time for walking.

The work proved to be harder than he had imagined. The grade-twelve history course alone was enough to keep a man busy – the history of Western Europe, Italy, Germany, France, England. And he had to prepare lessons in trigonometry, Latin, English, and chemistry. Fortunately Elaine was an unusually bright student, capable of doing most of the history by herself. Each of the fifteen students was on his or her own most of the time, and they all worked hard.

There were distractions.

The Hallowe'en dance, for instance.

"Of course, you're going," Frank said at dinner.

"I hadn't thought of it."

"Oh, you must," Jenny said. Then added, only half in jest, "It's the big social event of the fall."

"You're not kidding," Frank said. "They'll have that hall all dickied up with pumpkins and stocks of corn and strings of dried beans and all like that."

"Where do they find the stuff?"

"Oh, there's some gardens still growing. Bob Sanderson has a flowing well out there and he irrigates. Beautiful garden."

"I'd like to see it."

"Oh, you will," Jenny assured him. "Bob always has the teachers out for dinner at least twice a term. But you must go to the dance. People would never forgive you."

So on Friday evening he went to the dance, alone. Jenny and Frank had gone to the Fillmores' house for pre-dance drinks. They invited him, but he begged off. When he got to the dance in the town hall he realized immediately that most of the married couples there had imbibed a few before they came.

The hall was packed full when he arrived, the floor filled with dancers, the air with chatter and laughter. On benches along the sides of the hall were the grandparents and small children, the oldsters tapping their feet and gossiping, the youngsters wide-eyed and happy, skipping from group to group. More than one grandfather was dancing with a small grandchild and more than one grandmother was leading a blushing youth around the other dancers.

On the stage at the front sat the imported orchestra, a piano, a violin, a banjo, and two saxophones. They made up with gusto and noise what they lacked in finesse. The beat of "The Darktown Strutters' Ball" was filling the hall. The walls and ceiling were decorated with orange and black streamers and harvest vegetables. For a few hours the citizens of Harman were forgetting the Depression and the price of wheat and the dust and the grasshoppers. They were having themselves a time.

Every so often the blue-serge-suited youths would slip out the back door in twos and threes for a quiet swig of rye from the bottle; they returned with grins on their faces and renewed enthusiasm for the dance.

All the students from the school were there, and Hugh had the very definite feeling that he was under scrutiny. Jean McTavish came up to him leading a tall young man. Hugh realized with a shock that he had a harelip. It was partly covered with a blond moustache.

"This is my feller," Jean said. "Hugh, meet John Sanderson. John, this is Hugh."

They shook hands and John said, "I'm pleased to meet

you." His voice was only slightly affected by his harelip. Then he added, "Why don't you two go ahead and dance? I want to see Harry Telfer about a cow."

"Him and his cows," Jean said without annoyance. "They are never off his mind."

"Has he many?"

"Twenty-two exactly, not counting the calves and a ferocious bull. All pure-bred Jerseys. He's milking fifteen and every morning he brings the cans of that rich Jersey cream in to the station and ships them off to the Co-op Creamery in Saskatoon. This, along with the other farm work he does. When he gets enough cream money saved to add to what I can save from my miserable salary, well, we'll get married."

"I see."

"No, you don't. Maybe you will when you meet Bob Sanderson. John has worked hard enough to own two farms, but everything is in the old man's name."

"Sounds like a hard man."

"Hard, but honest and just - a justice of the peace, no less - and upright and religious and a bloody slave driver. I'll be so happy when John and Elaine can get away from him."

At the end of the dance she thanked him. "Maybe you can't sing, but you've sure got rhythm. Good luck with your duty dances."

So he dutifully danced with the mothers of his students and listened to their talk about their kids. He wanted desperately to dance with Elaine, but he wasn't sure it would be quite proper. But he watched her, dancing and laughing and having a great time. Her good spirits seemed to infect everyone with whom she came into contact. And then a ladies' choice was announced, and she came running over to him and took his hand and pulled him to his feet.

"Come on, Mr. Windmar," she said. "I've been waiting for this."

And so he took her in his arms and began a fox-trot.

She was light and easy in his arms and she smelled good. He had always been a good dancer and with her it was easy. She didn't lead, like some of the wives did; instead, she followed every move he made, easily and naturally. Soon his stiffness left him and he was dancing as he'd never danced before.

"You are a wonderful dancer," he said.

"You, too. I love to dance. I always thought I'd like to take lessons and be a ballet dancer. Does that sound crazy?"

"Nope. You'd be a wonderful ballet dancer. Why don't you?"

Her laugh rang out. "Oh, sure. Clear a space in the hayloft and take dancing by correspondence."

He had this overpowering urge to kiss her. To press her lithe, supple, young body close to his. So he drew back a little and his dancing became a bit stiff. But if she noticed she didn't say anything. And when the music stopped she made a little curtsey and said, "Thank you, kind sir," and was gone.

Later, when he was dancing with Jenny, who had a rather entrancing habit of putting her arm around his neck and playing with the hair on the back of his head, she said, "So you had a dance with poor Elaine."

"I can't think of anyone to whom the adjective 'poor' is less applicable."

"I only meant that she has to work so hard at home."

"Don't we all?"

"Yes, but you get paid for it."

"I suppose you could call it that."

She cuddled closer to him and attempted to steer him between two other couples.

"Let yourself go, for goodness sake. You'd be a good dancer if you'd just relax."

"Yes, Olive."

"Who's Olive?"

"My sister. She's always trying to tell me what to do, too."

"Oh. Well, pardon me for living." She was quiet for the

rest of the dance. When it was over he apologized to her, and she squeezed his hand. He wished she wouldn't squeeze his hand, but he realized that she'd had a drink or two of rye and ginger ale before she came and he forgave her.

He left early, walking alone across the weedy prairie to the Walpers' house. He could hear the orchestra pounding out "Hold That Tiger." More than anything else, he wanted to get drunk and make love to a woman, not necessarily in that order. Instead, he went back to his lonely room and his damned books and worked far into the night.

On Sunday morning he went to church. Frank had hinted that the good people of the district might talk if he didn't go to one church or another, and so he went to the United Church. The preacher, who held services in Harman in the morning and another town in the evening, was about forty-five, and fiercely intense. He made no bones about what he thought of the Depression. His text was based on the story of the loaves and fishes and he managed to turn it into a strong pitch for socialism.

As he talked, Hugh glanced around the pews at the grim-faced farmers in their blue serge suits, capitalists to a man, and he wondered how long the Reverend Henderson was going to get away with this pernicious talk.

When the service was over, Hugh paused at the door to shake hands with the reverend.

"You're the new principal," Henderson said. "I hear great things about you."

"Oh?"

"Conscientious and hard-working, that's what I hear on all sides. By the way, there's a political meeting in Saskatoon next month. Tommy Douglas and M.J. Coldwell will be there. I'll be driving in. Glad to give you a lift."

"I'm not much for politics."

"But, my dear boy, look about you. Men working their hearts out for practically nothing. You yourself should be getting three times what you are paid."

"They can barely afford to pay me what I am getting."

"That's just my point. That's why the system must be changed."

Hugh could see Alec Roarie watching him with a scowl on his face. "I'll let you know," he said, "and thanks."

As Hugh walked down the wooden sidewalk towards his boarding house, the chairman of the school board came up behind him and took him by the arm.

"Saw you talking to Henderson."

"Yes, I was."

"Trying to convert you to his Communist views, no doubt."

"Communist?"

"That's all those damned Crazy Calamity Farts are."

"Huh?"

"Isn't that what CCF stands for?"

"Hmm. . . . I wonder. If Christ were alive today, he might just join the party. After all, he said, 'Love thy neighbour as thyself.' "

"Well, he ain't, and if you want to save yourself a peck of trouble don't have nothing to do with those crazy bastards."

"You're happy with the way things are?"

"Of course I'm not. It's that Conservative government we got in Ottawa that's causing all this mess. Royal Bastard Bennett, the millionaire. 'Stead of farting around with those socialists, help to elect the Liberals. That's all we need."

"Is that what you do?"

"Damn betcha. It's Mackenzie King all the way."

"Well, you'll probably win, at that."

"Sure, and it's damned handy to be on the winning side. Take it from me. And this district's always been solid Liberal."

"I'll keep that in mind."

It snowed on November first and the long, cold, windy, unbelievably miserable prairie winter set in. Farmers put away their buggies and got out their cutters; automobile owners put their cars up on blocks and took the batteries into the house to keep them from freezing. Farmers drove their sleigh boxes into town to pick up their little supplies of relief coal. Many farmers were kept alive by direct relief from the municipality.

Frank Walper had little to do since few farmers had money for machinery. He spent much of his time in his basement workshop making decoys for duck-hunting. He and the lumber-yard agent and the postmaster took the train north to hunt moose, and returned with a good supply of meat. While he was away, Jenny had only the children and Hugh to care for. Hugh was glad that, during the long winter evenings, he was too busy to spend any time with her in the living room.

The children walked to school, rode horseback, or came in cutters. Many were pitifully underclothed. Hugh gave his good sheepskin jacket to Peter Zadunik, saying that it didn't fit him any more.

The schoolwork fell into a routine and Hugh devised little ways of making his work easier. But it still took all his free time to keep ahead of the students. He kept all his notes, tests, and other material in large looseleaf notebooks, one for each grade, in the sure knowledge that, with these, his job would be much easier next year.

Then he would have some time to write. He was storing away impressions, characters, and ideas for short stories. And he developed the trick of "What if?" What if he should be overcome with loneliness and have an affair with Jenny? What if he should fall in love with Elaine and get her pregnant? What if John Sanderson should murder his father? And so on and so on.

The rink was the social centre of the district. An ancient, sway-backed wooden curling rink with two sheets of ice was for the adults and the teenagers. Beside it was a large open-air rink for hockey and pleasure skating. On Friday evenings, the young people congregated there in bright, home-knitted sweaters and tuques and skated to the music of an old wind-up gramophone. They were marvellous skaters, gliding around the ice with easy rhythm, and in the centre the stunt men did leaps and figure eights. Leonard Green was a particularly adept skater and when he wasn't skating with Elaine he spent his time dazzling the spectators with his skill.

To his surprise and chagrin, Hugh found himself fiercely jealous of Leonard, because of the way he could skate and show off, and because of the way Elaine smiled at him and laughed with him and kidded with him.

It may have been his jealousy that caused his first problem at school. He found that, with most of his students, his threat of expulsion was unwarranted. These kids had a great ability to work by themselves and were eager to succeed. Hugh found himself becoming very fond of them. As time went on he spent time talking to them, urging them to greater excellence, and impressing upon them the importance of learning. He introduced them to the books of Hardy and Brontë and Mark Twain and Galsworthy and others. He joked with them, kidded them at times, and found that he had a certain talent for teaching. The students responded in kind.

All except Leonard Green. Leonard had that age-old teachers' complaint: a bad attitude. A tall, handsome boy, he seemed always to have a half sneer on his face. Hugh thought he was arrogant, supercilious, and mean. And he frequently came to class with his homework not done. Then, for three days in a row, he came late. Hugh told him that he was expelled until his father came to the school to talk to Hugh. Leonard merely grunted and left, waving goodbye to the others as he went out the door.

In less than half an hour Orville Green was at the door.

"Did you kick Leonard out?" he demanded in a loud voice.

"If you come back after four, we'll talk about it."

Green was a big, stout man; he was bald and had heavy shoulders. "We'll damned well talk about it now!"

Hugh stepped out into the hall and closed the classroom door. He could feel a tightness in his chest.

"I have work to do and this class has work to do and you are interfering with both. If you don't wish to talk to me after school, you can go to the chairman of the board."

Green looked at him with disgust. "Well, I damned well will. No two-bit teacher is going to kick my kid out and get away with it!"

Hugh went back into the room and closed the door. He could hear the farmer's heavy boots thumping down the hall; then the front door slammed.

Promptly at four o'clock Green was back at the school with Alec Roarie in tow. Roarie looked pained and uncomfortable. Mostly he wanted the school to run smoothly, with no problems.

"What happened?" he asked Hugh.

"He kicked my boy out of school and I ain't standing for it!" Green shouted.

"Shut up for a minute, Orville," Roarie said. "Hugh?"

"Well, it's very simple. We have a rule here that if any student can't comply with a few simple regulations he is expelled until I have a talk with one of his parents."

"You and your stupid rules," Green shouted.

"What rule did Leonard break?" Roarie asked.

"Not much. He's consistently late. And since he lives no farther from the school than many other students, I don't think it's unreasonable for him to be here at nine like the rest of them."

"Why can't he?" Roarie asked Green.

"Well, what's so all-fired important about a few minutes?"

"Now look, Orville," Roarie said. "Just see that he gets to school on time, eh?"

Green blew up. "I might have known you'd side with this pantywaist! Well, you ain't heard the last of it!" He stomped out of the room.

That evening at supper Frank grinned at Hugh across the table.

"Hear you had a run-in with Orville Green over Leonard," he said.

"How did you hear that?"

"All over town. Small place like this, everybody knows everything. They've already chosen up sides."

"Oh, my God."

"That Leonard always makes trouble," Jenny said.

"Good shortstop," Frank commented, cutting his round steak.

"What's that got to do with anything?"

"Nothing. Last Sports Day he was a kind of hero when he knocked a home run to win the game."

"I see."

Frank became serious. "That Orville is a real bad bastard. Talking in the pool-room about how he's going to run you out of the district. He'll stop at nothing."

"Six months' holidays twice a year," Tom scoffed, not unkindly. "You teachers sure have it made."

Hugh was home for the Christmas holidays. He'd been looking forward to it as a man on a desert island might look forward to being rescued. But now that he was home it was the same old thing. Bickering, one bathroom for seven people. People were poor in Harman, too, of course, but somehow in the city the poverty was more apparent. It heightened his hatred for Saskatchewan.

The preparations for Christmas at the school had been extensive. There was the Christmas concert in the town hall, with every last student participating. At first Hugh had stood aloof, but then he got into the spirit of things and coached the senior kids in some skits that ridiculed the rich bitches of Ontario. Any poking fun at Ontario got a big laugh. And at the dance that followed the concert, he'd managed to have another dance with Elaine, and the feel of her almost drove him crazy.

"You getting any nooky out there in the sticks?" Tom asked.

"Mind your own business."

"Remember what I said about staying out of those farm girls. They get pregnant if you hang your pants on their bedpost."

"Oh, you," Olive scoffed. "Think you know everything about girls. Don't pay any attention, Hugh."

Gwen was more interested in the social conditions at Harman. She had already mapped out for herself a career in anthropology.

Alvin was more interested in what was going on in Europe.

"There's going to be a war," he said. "Sure as hell there's going to be a war. That's what that madman Hitler is heading for, and England will bumble into it and we'll go right along. You'll see."

"I don't think so," Hugh said. "They can't be that crazy."

"Well, here's one guy they aren't going to get to fight their bloody war. Not by a damned sight!"

"You and Bertrand Russell, eh?"

"Damned right." His handsome face was agitated. "If nobody went to their damned war, they couldn't have one!"

"Oh, they'll go," Will said. "Just as they did last time. Just let the bands start playing; the people will cheer and the girls will pass out white feathers. They'll go. Besides, it's adventure. Chance to get away from the drudgery of home."

"What's this white-feather stuff?" Tom asked.

"That's what the women did in England, some of them. White feather means coward, and they sent them to men who were slow joining up."

"That's ridiculous," Gwen protested.

"Yep. But in wartime, everybody goes kind of crazy. Mass insanity, I call it," Will said.

Martha was too busy with her baby, Shawn, to be interested in much else. Shawn was a bright, sunny child and every member of the family doted on him. When people talked of war, Martha tended to pick him up and carry him to her room to read him nursery rhymes. Martha couldn't stand the thought of war. She remembered too well the bright young farm boys who went from their district to the first butchery and never returned. She had three sons of military age; only wee Shawn was safe.

Christmas Day was a success. Tom and Hugh bought small presents for everyone. Martha sewed new dresses for the girls. Alvin built a little wooden wheelbarrow for Shawn, who pushed it all day long. When Will was carving the turkey, Hugh noticed for the first time that he was getting old. There was grey in his hair; there were wrinkles on his hands. Hugh had always regarded his father as a tower of strength, but at forty-two, Will was beginning to show his age.

When Hugh went back to Harman he faced the three meanest months of the prairie winter. January, February, March: this was the testing time, when old horses died in the fields and old people died in their beds. The cold and the wind and the isolation were relentless. Almost everyone sank into a well of querulousness. Parents were short-tempered; children were nasty. Jean McTavish did her best to alleviate the situation by organizing reading clubs and dramatic readings and by directing the young people in plays.

The rink was even more the social centre of Harman. Those who didn't curl would sit in the tiny waiting room at the end of the rink, warmed by a pot-bellied stove, and comment on the games. The curlers, their breath like smoke, clapped their hands together and rubbed their ears and noses. Whenever anyone opened the door to the waiting room, a blast of cold air would hit the watchers and they would shout, "Shut that bloody door. Were you born in a barn?"

Hugh didn't go to the rink. With fierce determination he stayed in his little room under the eaves or in the school, which had a coal furnace, and prepared his lessons with great care and accuracy.

Forever afterwards when he thought of Saskatchewan he thought of that winter.

Occasionally he would be invited by one or another of his students' mothers to have Sunday supper with them. And once he went out to the Sanderson home.

It was March, and there was a break in the winter. The sun was high in the sky; the snow was melting and water dripped from the eaves. The roads had become impassable to cutter and buggy. Those who came to town mostly came on horseback.

It was on a Friday afternoon that Elaine came to his desk and asked if he would come to dinner.

"Yes, I'd like to. When?"

"This evening."

"But how will I get there? I'm afraid the road is impossible for walking."

"You can ride with me on Ginger. He often carries two." The way she smiled when she said this, Hugh knew he was being given some kind of a test. "You can ride, can't you?"

"Yeah. Sure. Of course."

So after school, with many of his students looking on, Hugh waited on the school steps while Elaine went to the barn for her horse. She rode him to the steps beside Hugh.

"Jump on quickly," she ordered.

Hugh had never ridden bareback in his life, but he wasn't going to admit that. He jumped on the horse behind Elaine.

"Put your arms around my waist and hang on," she directed as Ginger bolted for the gate and onto the road. The audience gave a little cheer as Hugh hung on for dear life.

He had a good sense of balance and was in little danger of falling off, but immediately he was confronted with another problem. The closeness of Elaine – he was tight against her bum – and the motion of the galloping horse, and the feel of her waist just above his clutching hands, combined to give him an erection.

Because of the way horses are built, his erect penis was tight against her. There was no way of moving back. And as the horse galloped, Elaine's rump rubbed up and down on the front of his penis. He was sure Elaine could feel what was going on, but there was nothing she could do about it, either. Just before they reached the farm, Hugh went off in his underwear.

And now he confronted an even bigger problem: what do to about it. He knew that the long, fleece-lined drawers he was wearing would absorb most of the mess. And luckily, when they reached the front porch of the house, John was waiting on the step. Hugh muttered, "Bathroom," and John led him up the stairs and showed him the bathroom. Hugh dashed in, latched the door, sat down on the chemical toilet, and cursed all horses, nubile young ladies, and life in general.

There was a small commode in the room with a huge porcelain basin in which sat a porcelain jug filled with water. Hugh found that the heavy underwear had indeed protected his trousers, but there was nothing for it but to remove the underwear. But what to do with the drawers? He surveyed the bathroom desperately. There was a large tin bathtub on legs, and he realized that if he stuffed the drawers far under they might not be discovered for some time. And then whoever discovered them might think they belonged to one of the teen-aged Sanderson boys. At least Hugh hoped so.

He felt chilly without the long, warm drawers, which he had been wearing since November, but considered himself lucky to get out of his predicament.

Downstairs, Elaine and two other Sanderson girls were in the kitchen, busy with preparations for the meal. John invited Hugh to inspect the farm. And so they went outside, stepping gingerly between puddles and piles of slush mixed with cow manure, while the March breeze playfully caressed Hugh's legs and genitals.

The barn was big and filled with cows, horses, pigs, and cats. Hugh noticed with surprise that one of the cats was busy chewing on a red, veined object that looked like a testicle.

"We've been nutting some pigs," John explained, then led him along the line of Jersey cows, pausing here and there to lean on a cow's haunches and give her name and milking record. “This one won first prize at the Saskatoon Exhibition last year. I’d really like to take her to the Royal Winter Fair in Toronto. Show those eastern snobs a thing or two.”

“Why do you think an Ontario farmer is any more of a snob than a Saskatchewan farmer?”

“You’re right, Hugh. Just a habit we westerners have got into.”

John showed off a mean-looking Jersey bull that glared at them with scorn and animosity. “His name is Napoleon,” John said, “and he sure can handle these cows.”

Hugh looked around at the warm, fecund barn, reeking with sex, and wondered what John and Jean did in here. The place was ripe with it. In one of the empty stalls a big brindle tomcat had mounted a she. He had his teeth locked into the skin on the back of her neck and was clawing the floor with his hind feet as he thrust home.

“Looks like we’ll have some more kittens soon,” John remarked casually.

At five-thirty, as Hugh was inspecting John’s milk house with absolutely no interest, there was a clanging sound from the back door.

“Soup’s on,” John said, and when they emerged into the late-afternoon sunlight Hugh saw one of the Sanderson kids banging on a metal triangle that hung by the kitchen door.

Inside there was a tantalizing smell of roast turkey, and when they sat down to dinner, Bob Sanderson was there at the end of the table, looking like a feudal lord. Ranged along both sides of the table were children of all ages. Elaine and two of her sisters brought bowls of potatoes, carrots, and gravy from the kitchen. Hugh noticed that although Elaine had been working steadily since they got home, she had found time to change into a charming dress and to comb her hair. She looked beautiful.

When the girls had taken their places near the kitchen, and Hugh and John had seated themselves on either side of Bob, the father bowed his head and spoke in a clear, strong voice.

"For what we are about to receive, Oh Lord, make us truly thankful. Amen." Then he beamed at his clan. "You know, Mr. Windmar," he said with a huge smile, "everything on this table was produced on this farm - milk, butter, vegetables, turkey, even the wheat for the bread. Except the sugar and salt and pepper, of course." He began carving the turkey and the serious business of eating began.

The food was marvellous, and Hugh forgot the minor irritations he'd suffered since leaving the school. The young Sandersons said nothing during the meal, glancing at Hugh shyly from time to time with lowered heads.

When they had finished their meal and the apple pie that followed, the young Sandersons excused themselves one by one and left the table. They all had chores to do that would keep them busy until bedtime.

Elaine and her sisters cleared the table and began the dishes, while the three men moved into the living room. Bob Sanderson lighted a pipe, and Hugh offered John one of his Turrets.

When they had lit up, Bob Sanderson said, "Well, young man, how are you getting along in our fair district?"

"Not too badly, I think."

"My children think you are - I believe their phrase is 'the cat's whiskers.' "

"I'm pleased to hear it."

"Nothing like a good education, I say."

"I agree. I hope that Elaine can continue hers after she finishes grade twelve."

"If she passes."

"Oh, she'll pass all right. She has a quick mind and a determination to do well." He was sounding as much like a school principal as he could manage.

"Yeah, she's a lot like her mother that way." Bob Sanderson looked sad for a minute. "And I don't know what I'd have done without her. All these children to raise."

Hugh happened to glance at John; on the oldest son's face was an expression of disgust and contempt. The old hypocrite, Hugh thought. And he thought of Elaine tied to this household, growing old as she mothered this bunch of kids. Someone should rescue her. And then he remembered Tom's admonition: "Don't let yourself get mixed up with some lush young farm girl. You'll be hooked good."

Chapter Thirteen

"Don't let yourself get hooked, little brother." As Hugh drove along the highway towards Harman, Tom's words kept running through his mind. Well, he never had let himself be hooked. He had known plenty of women since Elaine and had enjoyed their company, but somehow they'd all fallen short of his expectations.

Another phrase haunted his mind, one from his teaching days, from the play *Julius Caesar*. Just before the Battle of Philippi, Brutus says to his fellow conspirator Cassius, "There is a tide in the affairs of men, which, taken at the flood, leads on to fortune; omitted, all the voyage of their life is bound in shallows and in miseries."

Had he missed the full flood? His mind went back to two years after Elaine had graduated. He had fallen in love with her. Even now the memory stirred his innards. He remembered returning from Saskatoon to face his third year in that desolate town.

It was dry that September, desperately dry; there was practically no rain. The wheat crops were a pitiful mess, stunted and grasshopper-ridden. Few farmers were driving cars and there was little for Frank to do. He hung around the house a lot, went on extended hunting trips, and left Jenny alone with the children - and Hugh.

The Walpers needed his board money. And, although he knew malicious tongues were beginning to wag, he decided to continue living with them.

But nothing seemed to be going right. Hugh had kept going in the first year by reminding himself that he'd got a good job in the midst of the Depression; in the second year, the mind-boggling work of preparing lessons for four high-school grades and the status of his job had helped. Now all that was gone. Nothing remained but day after day of drudgery in the classroom, the nerve-wracking business of policing and keeping ahead of a room full of active minds. Some natural-born teachers, he knew, relished the challenge, but he wasn't a natural-born teacher. His inclination now was to say, "To hell with them. If they don't want to learn, that's up to them."

He preferred to concentrate on his own writing. But the conditions at the school were so uninspiring he found writing almost impossible. And so he got into trouble. Trouble with Leonard and his crazy father. Trouble with Jenny Walper.

One thing many people didn't mention when talking about the Depression was the mind-destroying boredom of life. Stuck in one place with the same people, no money for travelling or having fun, endless days of wind and dust, drab food, and thread-bare clothing, all contributed to boredom. And when people are bored, they tend to get into trouble.

Frank coped with boredom by doing what he'd always done, playing cards in the back of the Chinese restaurant in winter, playing baseball in the summer, hunting in the fall.

Jenny could do none of these things. So she set out to seduce Hugh. During the long evenings when Frank was away and the boys were in bed and she and Hugh were together in the house, she became obsessed with the idea of getting him into her bed. She pretended a great interest in literature and read the books he loaned her, especially the books by Thomas Hardy. Although Hardy was a Victorian writer, his books were ripe with sex. Not the modern kind of sex, where couples get into bed at the first meeting and try all kinds of experiments, but something much more subtle and steamy and arousing. Sex that left a great deal to her imagination.

It was *Far from the Madding Crowd* that finally did it,

that and the drinking. How was he to know that after a couple of drinks she would go wild? They had been discussing the scene where Sergeant Troy is demonstrating the art of swordsmanship. The boys were sleeping at a friend's house; Frank was away on a hunting trip; and there the two of them were. They were at the best part of the scene when Jenny excused herself and went upstairs. When she came down she had on a long frilly dressing gown, and as she reached the bottom step she undid the rope that held it shut and let it slip to the floor. She was naked.

Jenny had a nice, tight little figure with good breasts and the sight of it was too much for Hugh.

Afterwards, naked in the big bed upstairs, she said, "You aren't very experienced, are you?"

"Believe it or not, this is my first time."

"You catch on fast," she said with a chuckle, and pulled him to her. Most of the night they enjoyed each other until Hugh could perform no more. And then they went to sleep.

Hugh awoke next morning and found himself alone in the big bed. He could hear Jenny downstairs preparing breakfast and singing softly to herself. He was overcome not with remorse or guilt or shame, but with fear. Sheer panic. Frank was big and strong and had a terrible temper. He could, Hugh realized, break Hugh in half if he wished. The other feeling that overcame him was hunger. He was starving. Fear and hunger, he knew, were two of the strongest of all human urges. Hunger won out, and he went downstairs to breakfast.

Jenny greeted him cheerfully, much as she always did. No blushes, no intimate little pats, no kisses. Business as usual. And it dawned upon Hugh that she had put the incident out of her mind. Like a lot of good people, she had the capacity for forgetting, literally forgetting anything that upset her. Not that it might not happen again. Given the same circumstances it easily could, and probably would.

But then Hugh further complicated his life by falling in love. It happened that same weekend, and he always thought one incident had something to do with the other.

Later that morning he was having his regular walk with Jean when she said, "Why don't you come to the Young Peoples' meeting after church tomorrow evening?"

"And play parlour games and have deep discussions?"

"You really are a snob, do you know that?"

"Probably."

"You might actually have some fun. It's out at the Sandersons' this time, and they always have a marvellous lunch." She walked in silence for a moment. "Besides, it will get you out of the Walpers' house."

"What does that mean?"

She stopped and turned to him. "Hugh, in a town the size of Harman, everybody keeps track of everything. It's practically their only recreation. They know you and Jenny are alone in that house night after night."

"You're telling me to move?"

"Well, I suppose I deserve that, but I'm not going to stop. I think you should come to the meeting and flirt a little, with Maggie Jones, for instance. She's a sort of clearing house for all town and country gossip."

"Naturally, being the telephone operator."

"Listen here, Hugh. I'm your friend and I'm trying to help you."

"I'm sorry, Jean. I know. Okay. Young Peoples' meeting after church tomorrow evening. How do I get there?"

"You can drive out with John and me."

"You're damned lucky, you know. To have John, I mean. Keeps you from dying of boredom."

"And from gossip. You see, we've been going together for so long that we're not a hot item any more. Not like. . . ."

"Jenny Walper and me."

"Oh, stop it. Gossip can be a terrible thing. I know there's nothing to it, but. . . ."

"How do you know that?"

"Well – you're not the type."

"No fire? No passion? You read Somerset Maugham?"

"Of course."

"Well, then you know you never can tell. That's his one great theme - in "The Letter," "Cakes and Ale," all of them. You never know what fire burns beneath the most placid surface. Never know when the volcano may erupt."

She stopped again and looked at him. "Are you having an affair with Jenny Walper?"

"No."

"I thought not. You are too, well, too honourable."

"Thank you."

"But this town. How I hate it. Do you know we are probably being watched right now?"

"How?"

"Old Everet Sharn. He can see in all directions from that little cupola on top of his house, and he has a powerful spyglass."

"And he watches people?"

"Constantly. Not only that, but he prowls around at night peeking in windows."

Hugh felt a shiver of fear. "He does?"

And that's what finally made him decide to attend the Young Peoples' meeting at the Sandersons' farm.

Jenny was surprised and somewhat miffed. "Do you think you'll really have any fun with those yokels?"

My God, Hugh thought, she's already assuming a proprietary attitude towards me.

"Part of my job, really," he said.

"You've never considered it so before."

He let that one pass. And after church, during which the minister made another strong pitch for the CCF cause, Hugh drove with Jean and John to the Sandersons' farm. There were about twenty young people at the meeting, many of whom Hugh had seen occasionally at church. Elaine, as befits the hostess, appeared to be in charge, and when the meeting was called to order Hugh was surprised to discover that she was also the president. They didn't play parlour games, but after the reading of the minutes of the previous meeting they got into a serious discussion about "the responsibilities of the church for the physical as well as the spiritual welfare of the people." It was led by Reverend Henderson and very quickly took a political turn; people used phrases like "poverty in the midst of plenty" and "the vested interest." To his surprise, Hugh found himself defending the status quo and his chief opponent was Elaine. He noticed that she had matured a lot since leaving school, and was even more attractive than he remembered.

Leonard Green was there and he sat beside Elaine - too damned close, Hugh figured - and sided with her in the debate. This caused Hugh to take a stronger position than he otherwise would have.

"The trouble with your planned economy, as you call it, is that the planners always get carried away. They want to plan everything."

"What's wrong with that?" Leonard wanted to know.

"Well, what's wrong with it is that it means the end of individual freedom. And you have a situation such as they have in Russia."

"There's no unemployment in Russia," Leonard shot back.

"It seems to me," Reverend Henderson said eagerly, "that what you have said doesn't necessarily follow. We are talking about democratic socialism, not dictatorship. The kind they have in Sweden. Production for use rather than production for profit."

"You take away the profit motive and you take away competition and you remove most of the spice of life," Hugh countered.

John spoke up. "I agree with that. I know things are bad now, damned bad, but a few good rains could make a big difference."

"That's ridiculous, John," Elaine said, her face flushed with excitement. "What good will rain do? Only produce more wheat, and we're losing money on every bushel we grow now. Don't you see?" she went on. "There are young people who want children and are afraid to have them. People who need houses, money to educate their children. This is where your competition has brought us. We need co-operation, not competition!"

"What we need is a good war," her younger brother Clifford put in. "That'll bring back prosperity."

As the debate went on, the Reverend Henderson was ecstatic. "This is marvellous," he said to Hugh at lunch time. "Absolutely marvellous. Young people talking about things that matter." He patted Hugh on the shoulder. "You will see the light. More joy in heaven, you know."

The lunch consisted of pork sandwiches, made with home-made bread, and cookies and cake. There was some excellent Cheddar cheese, part of a shipment of free food from Ontario. The Reverend Henderson prayed over the food, but found it difficult to thank God for it. The Depression was hard on Protestant preachers.

Hugh managed to sit beside Elaine at lunch.

"Do you really believe those things you said, Mr. Windmar?" she asked.

"Not entirely. But in my family, everyone argues constantly about everything. I usually take the losing side just to sort of balance things up. And by the way, my name is Hugh."

"Hugh. Seems funny to call you that after being one of your students."

"I'm not that ancient, you know, not much older than you."

"That's right. Would you like to go to a dance?"

"A dance? Why, yes."

"There's a harvest dance in Willow Lake next Friday night. John is taking Jean. They asked me to come along. Would you like to come, too?" She said it so naturally and without any sort of guile that he answered in kind.

"You bet I would. How do we get there?"

"Dad's car."

"Great!" Something to do. Some excitement. A relief from boredom. "I'll see if I can get a crock."

"That would be nice."

A "crock" was a twenty-six-ounce bottle of rye whisky, the standard Canadian drink. Since there were no cocktail lounges or bars, most drinking was done in cars, straight from the bottle.

All that week Hugh thought of the dance. But then, on Wednesday at noon, Jenny said to him, "Frank and I are going to the dance in Willow Lake on Friday. Would you like to come with us?"

"Uh, thanks . . . but I'm going with John Sanderson."

"Oh, indeed. How nice. And Elaine?"

"Yeah. As a matter of fact, she invited me."

"Well." She got up from the table and busied herself at the sink.

"That Elaine's become quite a looker," Frank said. "Damned nice girl, too."

Jenny's small, pert mouth was set in a straight line. "Yes, she'll be looking for a husband."

Hugh managed to get a bottle of rye whisky from Pop, who, since there was no liquor store in Harman, doubled as a bootlegger.

There was a full moon that Friday night. A harvest moon. Big as a house and red, sitting on the horizon. When Hugh got into the back seat of Bob Sanderson's Essex sedan with Elaine beside him, he felt a shiver of excitement.

And as he sat close to Elaine, feeling the essence of her, he was a boy again. Not a school principal, straight-laced and prissy, but a reckless, fun-loving schoolboy. More than anything, he wanted to pull this girl to him and kiss her hard, and strangely he knew that she wanted it, too.

It was about fifty miles to Willow Lake and when they reached the dance hall it was surrounded by cars, mostly ancient. From inside they could hear the sound of saxophones, sweet and mellow. When John had parked the car, Hugh said, "Perhaps we should have a small libation before going in."

"Great idea." John laughed. "I'd like a drink, too."

And so they each had a snort from the bottle. Elaine and Jean barely took a sip, but John and Hugh took a couple of good swallows. The raw liquor burned all the way down to Hugh's stomach and permeated his entire body.

Hugh could never remember much about that dance, except holding Elaine tight in his arms. There were no parents of students there requiring "duty dances," nobody they knew. Jenny and Frank never did arrive. Frank explained later that Jenny had developed one of her violent headaches, which suited Frank fine because he hated dancing anyway; he much preferred a card game in the back of Pop's restaurant.

Hugh and John made a couple of trips to the car for more to drink while the women powdered their noses.

Hugh didn't dance with Jean, but it didn't matter, as she and John seemed to be in a world of their own. When the dance was over they got back into the car for the long trip home. As Elaine snuggled up to Hugh he bent over and kissed her on the lips, and she responded eagerly.

"I've been wanting to do that ever since I first saw you!" she murmured in his ear.

"You have?"

"I used to sit in class and look at you when you were teaching and dream about you kissing me. And when you leaned over me to help me with my trig, well, I nearly died."

"Me, too," he lied. It was the first of many lies he would tell her.

As he thought of it now, driving towards Harman, he mused as he had many times that this girl had been like a precious jewel, rare and natural. His lack of experience with girls and his one experience with Jenny Walper had blinded him to her rare qualities.

During the next term, Hugh spent all his spare time with Elaine. Bob Sanderson did nothing to encourage him, being loath to lose his free housekeeper and a surrogate mother for his children. But Elaine was a strong, determined woman. She was deeply in love and never hesitated to say so.

As for Hugh, he too was in love, but his naturally cautious nature prevented him from admitting it to himself or anyone else.

There was a "salesman's suite," scarcely ever used, in the old ramshackle hotel, and Hugh persuaded the proprietress, Mrs. Simpson, to rent it to him.

When he told Jenny he was going to move out, she looked at him accusingly.

"Well, if you're not happy here you might as well leave," she said.

"It's not that I haven't been happy here. It's just that – "

"I'm sorry if the service hasn't been satisfactory." She emphasized the word "service" and turned away.

Frank was more sympathetic. "I can see why you want a place of your own," he said. "But you're going to get damned sick of Pop's cooking. Besides, you'll never get away with it."

"Huh?"

"Not in this town. Never in a thousand years. But good luck."

From the radio in Tom's Buick came a girl's voice singing, "What would I give to bring back those old times?"

What would he give? Even now he wondered. In 1936 and 1937 he had wanted, more than anything else, to be a successful writer. Now he was a successful writer. Known and respected throughout the country, approved by some, detested by others, as any good playwright should be. Would he give that up to bring back those old times? In the videotape of his mind, the Depression years always appeared as a big black blob – except for that one winter and spring. They were an oasis, with soft music and tender love.

Elaine came to his apartment often, though she knew that her father and the community disapproved strenuously. It wasn't that love had made her blind. She knew the price and was willing to pay it. She sewed curtains for his windows and painted pictures for his walls. Hugh bought a record player and the room was full of music, classical and modern. He had a great enthusiasm for the singing of the fine Irish tenor John McCormack and had most of his records.

They played house in that apartment. Often Elaine would bring hot meals from the farm and Hugh kept a stock of cheap wine on hand. Nine hundred dollars went a long way in 1937. Elaine would drop in at odd times, often late at night, and sometimes she wouldn't go home until morning. For, truth to tell, this nineteen-year-old girl, full of love and devotion, looked upon herself as a married woman, which she was sure she soon would be.

They made love joyfully and without caution. Elaine gave herself to love-making completely. Since she was his first love, Hugh assumed that all women behaved so. But she was the only woman Hugh was ever to know who laughed during the act. Her orgasms were a sigh rather than a violent threshing, and she was never petulant or mean.

In this idyllic state, Hugh let his school work go to pot. He got by with the notes he'd made the first two years, and didn't add to them. He ignored the discipline at school. When Miss Anderson sent him a small, scrawny child who had stolen ten cents from another student, Hugh gave the boy a quarter and told him not to steal any more.

"He should be punished," the primary teacher said, her thin lips tightening with indignation. "How will he learn right from wrong?"

"Is it right that he should have no decent winter clothing? That his lunch should consist of cold boiled potatoes and withered carrots?"

"That has nothing to do with it. Stealing is a crime and a sin."

"Tell that to the money barons in Ontario and the bankers who are stealing these people blind."

"Oh!" She flounced out of the room.

Jean was more direct. "Have you any idea what you are doing to Elaine and to your career?"

"Career? Are you kidding? You call this a career?"

"What about Elaine? Why don't you two get married? It would solve everything."

He turned away.

"I know it's none of my business, but - "

"That's right."

He ignored all the signs. He was active and happy. He began writing short stories again and sending them off to

Liberty Magazine and getting rejection slips in return. He caught Elaine's enthusiasm for the CCF party, and the two of them went with the Reverend Henderson to meetings in drafty, cold, ill-equipped one-roomed schoolhouses where ragged farmers sat in baffled silence and listened glumly while Henderson told them that with a planned economy all would be well.

"You do all the work while somebody in a big office in Toronto reaps all the profits. They sow not, neither do they spin. They manipulate a few figures and make millions, while you lose your farms to the banks. Five families have moved from this district in the past five years. Where will it end? You have the power, if you will but use it." The good reverend became very heated in his enthusiasm. Why, he wondered, do they keep on voting Liberal at a time like this?

Elaine was a sincere speaker and talked movingly of the young people caught in this economic trap. Hugh made a half-hearted attempt to describe what was happening to education because of the Depression, but he couldn't bring himself to use the catch phrases. He was there because Elaine was there, and the long cutter rides over rutted snow trails gave him a chance to cuddle with her under the warm buffalo robe.

And then the blow-up came. Like a volcanic mountain, the district had been smouldering subterraneously and then, in March, it erupted.

It was a beautiful March that year, the kind of spring that comes rarely in the prairies. After the long, dull, cold, windy winter, the returning sun really means liberation to Saskatchewan farmers. The pastures begin to show patches of grass; on the hillsides, purple crocuses sprout. Gophers come out of their holes and sit up and chirp their welcome to spring. The crows, the first birds to return north, wing slowly overhead and caw greetings to the people they've left behind. Manure piles melt and steam, the frozen slops by the back door thaw and are carried off by water from the roofs. It is the return of life - and a great time for making snowballs.

Elaine and Hugh had just returned from a long Sunday stroll on the railroad tracks, the only dry place to walk. They had made snowballs with the softening snow and pelted each other. They had laughed and played and kissed, and along with every living thing, they welcomed the return of the sun.

They got back to the apartment and shoved up the one window to let in the March wind when there was a knock on the door. It was Alec Roarie, standing glumly in the hall.

"Hello, Alec," Hugh said. "Isn't this a lovely day?"

"I don't feel so lovely."

"Something wrong?"

"Everything's wrong. People are up in arms."

"Oh, they're always complaining."

"Don't I know it? What did you ever do to Jenny Walper?"

"Why, nothing."

"She's sure after your hide. Maybe it's because you moved out."

"Hmm . . . what's she saying?"

"That you ain't fit to teach her kids."

"They're not in my room."

"Same difference. She says you ain't fit to teach anybody's kids. Green's hot, too. Ain't forgot how you kicked Leonard out."

"To hell with them."

"Well, maybe. But they've insisted we call a special board meeting for next Monday. You be there?"

"Why?"

"Defend yourself against these morality charges."

"Oh, my God. Jenny Walper talking morality!"

"Yep. Some of the others are upset about your political activity. Say a teacher shouldn't concern himself with politics."

"What do you think, Alec?"

"I figure you got a right to do what you want in that line, and your private life is your own affair. But. . . ."

"But?"

"Well, from what I hear, things aren't going too well at school, either."

"What in hell do they know about what should go on in school? I don't tell these women how to do their housework or raise their kids: they don't tell me how to teach!"

"Take it easy. Save it for the meeting."

The meeting, as Hugh remembered it, was a shambles. After a long Saskatchewan winter, everybody was irritable and pugnacious. Now they closed ranks against the outsider. They were careful not to make any direct accusations, but they hinted that they wanted his immediate resignation.

The school board, however, absolutely refused to fire him. Hugh assumed an attitude of aloof contempt, which infuriated everybody. But when it came down to making a definite statement, not one of them was prepared to bell the cat. And so the meeting ended in a stalemate.

When he got back to his room after the meeting, Elaine was waiting for him. Hugh was still angry and disgusted.

"Well," he said, "I didn't expect to see you here."

"Why not?" Her face showed surprise and hurt.

"Well. . . ."

"You thought I would join that pack of jackals?"

"Of course not, but this is your home. They're your people."

"My home, but not my people. You are my people now. Where thou goest, I go."

His response to that should have been to take her in his arms and make love to her. But rather than reassure him, her words frightened him.

"Let's go for a walk, a long walk," he said. "Got to get the stench of that meeting out of my nostrils."

So they went for a long walk. He walked her home, in fact, but didn't go in. And then Hugh became angry. Furious that people of such low intelligence and lack of sensibility should have any effect on his life. That he should be having anything to do with them at all. Dull clods, philistines, unimaginative, unfeeling dolts. He decided to get out, whatever the cost.

And then fate took a hand. Hugh had always imagined that a pernicious machine in magazine publishers' offices took stories out of envelopes and placed them in self-addressed envelopes, along with rejection slips. Somehow that machine failed to function: he got a letter of acceptance from *Liberty Magazine* and a cheque for a thousand dollars.

Nothing that ever happened to him had affected him so much. As he stared at the cheque, tears welled in his eyes. The money represented emancipation - more than emancipation, freedom. He knew he would go to Toronto and become a writer. He let out a whoop and a holler and rushed over to the store, where he pulled Alec Roarie from a step ladder, from which he was arranging mens' work shirts on a shelf.

"What's up, Hugh?" the chairman asked.

"I'm quitting, that's what's up!"

"Come on. This thing will blow over. Several people have mentioned to me what a good teacher you are. It's just a few - "

"Screw them. Screw them all!"

"Hey, take it easy."

"Not you, Alec. I appreciate what you've done and I appreciate you as a friend. But the rest of them - well, look here!" He showed Alec the cheque.

Alec whistled. "A thousand big ones for a story!"

"Yep. And there's a lot more where that came from. I'm going to Toronto and become a writer."

"But Toronto is full of unemployed people."

"Nope, not now. Depression's easing off in the east. It's not just this. I've never liked this goddamned province. Nothing here but farmers and businessmen, and I'm neither. I'm a writer, goddamn it, a writer!"

When he told Elaine she laughed with glee. "I knew you

could do it. I always knew it! When do we leave?"

So this was it. The moment he had always secretly dreaded.

"Well, Elaine," he said. "It's going to be awfully tough there in Toronto. Getting started, I mean."

She looked at him more in sorrow than in anger. "You don't want me to go with you, do you?"

"Not just at first. I'll send for you when I become established."

"Yes, of course. You must be free to do your writing. That's the important thing."

He could see that she was terribly hurt. Suddenly brought down from her cloud of ecstasy to face reality.

She left him then. They never did celebrate his great success. He submitted his resignation and, for the last month of the term, threw himself into his school work, determined that every one of his students should pass.

Then, one day after school in mid-June, just before final exams were to commence, Jean McTavish came into his room. Her Scottish eyes were flashing. She stood in front of his desk, hands on the edge of it, leaning towards him.

"What's up?" he asked.

"Did you know that Elaine may be pregnant?"

"My God! Of course I didn't!"

"Well, she thinks she is. Made me promise not to tell you."

"How did you find out?"

"Oh God, you men. Blind, blind, blind."

"She never said anything."

"Of course not. And ruin your great career?" She flung her hands high in an exaggerated gesture. "You really don't know anything about this girl, do you?"

"What do you want me to do?"

"What do I want you to do? What does Elaine want you to do? The point is, what do you want to do? And you mustn't tell her I told you."

What would his life have been like if he had married her and taken her with him? He knew she would have gone, and he knew that they would have made it together. But poverty and depression had ground him down, and the thought of a wife and child was too much.

And so he left her. Her last words to him on the station platform as he held her tight were, "Goodbye, Hughie, my darling. Don't you worry about me. I'll be fine. It's you I'm worried about. May God help and protect you."

The train pulled out and he waved to her through the window. A small, erect figure, smiling her big, broad smile and blowing him kisses. And as soon as that train began to move, his thoughts left the past and concentrated on the future. His future. Everybody has a right to a chance.

"I have an uncle in Toronto," Martha said when he got back to Saskatoon. "He's an executive with the Massey-Harris company. He may be able to help. I'll write him."

"Don't bother, please."

"It's too bad my parents have moved away." Martha shook her head sadly. Martha's parents had left Toronto shortly after they lost everything in 1929. They had an apartment in Antigonish and Dr. O'Neil treated the children of impoverished fishermen.

Tom was surprisingly philosophical. "It's a damned tough thing you're planning to do, little brother, but I guess everybody's gotta do what they gotta do. Me, I like this place just fine. Saskatchewan won't always have drought and misery. You'll see. He rubbed his big face with his hand. "And don't starve. I can always spare a few bucks, you know. Besides, when you're a famous writer, I can always say I helped." He laughed his good-natured laugh and they shook hands.

William Henry was pensive. "Ontario, eh? You know, I've never been back since I left in 1912. Always meant to, but never got around to it. It's a grand place."

Olive said, "Just see that you don't become one of those damned snooty easterners."

Gwen, going into her final year of high school and excelling in all her courses, was already thinking of her own emancipation. "I know you'll succeed," she said. "You know how to."

"Toronto, oh Toronto," Martha said. "How I would like to go with you. Maybe some day, when this wretched Depression is over. . . ."

But Alvin was the one who most wanted to go. "You sure are taking a chance leaving a good job in these times. Wish to hell I could go with you."

"Maybe," Hugh told him vaguely. "When I'm established, I'll see if there are any jobs you could do."

"Yeah, sure."

They all went down to the station to see him off, and as the train pulled out, Hugh watched them waving to him, then he sank back in his seat. The train was heading in the direction he wanted to go, and he hoped he might never see this place again.

Chapter Fourteen

"How's Ma?" Tom asked.

"She's sleeping, I think. I certainly hope so." Olive was sitting alone in the living room. She was tired.

"Where's everybody?"

"Gwen and Shawn are downtown arranging for the funeral."

"Funny how the old man died, just like that."

"Funny?"

"You know what I mean, Olive. So sudden. At least he didn't suffer any. I'll settle for that when my turn comes. A quick heart attack in the morning and poof, gone, all she wrote."

"Yes. Just like that. And Mother won't be far behind. The shock almost killed her. I never saw anybody go down so fast."

"Natural. They were part of each other. One part dies and the other, well. . . ."

"Did you manage to reach Hugh?"

"No, he's on the road somewhere. Should have put a phone in that car. Is Ma all right, do you think?"

"As good as can be expected. I think her mind is slipping, but it's hard to tell with the tranquillizers. Talks about Alvin all the time, about when he was born on the homestead and the time he wandered into the hayfield and Dad just missed cutting his legs off with the mowing machine."

"I remember that. Alvin was what you might call accident-prone."

"But she's talking about him as though he might walk into the room any time."

"Maybe he will."

"What?"

"Well, you know what they say. When you die you meet your old friends."

"Do you really think we do?"

"Search me. Nobody's ever come back to tell us about it."

"God, how I envy you."

"How's that?"

"The straightforward way you accept everything. No pondering, no worries, no sense of guilt."

"If you say so, sister. Well, I gotta go. I'll go up and see Ma for a minute. See if I can cheer her up. Anything I can do for you?"

"No. I mean, no thanks."

"We do appreciate it, you know, everything you're doing for Ma." He walked across the room and laid a hand lightly on her shoulder.

She seized his hand and held it. "I know you do. You and I have held the fort all these years while the rest went away. It's the least we can do for Ma after all the things she did for us."

"Yeah." He patted the hand that was holding his and went out of the room and up the stairs. Martha was propped up in bed, in a frilly blue bed jacket.

"Hi there, how's my number-one girl?" Tom said as he sat down on the bedside chair and took her thin white hand in his big one.

"Oh, it's you, Tom. Do you think he will come? Alvin, I mean?" It was little more than a whisper.

"Could be. You never know."

"It was all that girl's fault, you know. All her fault." Tears trickled down the wrinkled cheeks and she turned her head away and closed her eyes.

Was it the girl's fault? Or was it Hitler's, or Chamberlain's, or the fault of the signers of the Treaty of Versailles?

Or was it Alvin's own fault, Tom wondered. Who could assess the blame?

Alvin had been twenty-one years old in 1939. He had never had a job or owned a car or paid for a ride on a train. He hadn't even had a girl. He had a half-dozen scribblers filled with poems, which he never showed to anyone. He was a tall, skinny man, wiry and strong. He helped Martha in the house, doing the wash in the old wringer washing machine in the basement, waxing the worn floors in the living room and skating around on them in his stockinged feet to give them a shine. He peddled homemade marmalade on the street and he never had more than two dollars in his pants pocket at one time. He bought Turret cigarettes for one cent each from the drugstore; the druggist took them out of a tin box known as a "flat fifty." Sometimes he sat in the back room at the drugstore and played bridge with Alec and Joe and Myron; they had been in high school with him and were also unemployed. A few times they bought Connor's kippered snacks and crackers; they would sit on a bench in the park and eat them. Joe and Myron were in the naval reserves and every Tuesday night they went to the old naval barracks downtown for what they jokingly called "training." Alvin had tried to join, but the chief petty officer at the barracks said the reserves weren't taking on any more men.

The other three called Joe a bullshitter. He would make up the most outlandish stories and swear they were true. According to him, he'd been in a fight in Hong Kong and had the scar to show for it, had mushed over the frozen north, had lived with a girl on the Hawaiian islands. The others knew he was making things up and when they said so he would swear the stories were true. But his adventures were over when he fell between the cars of a freight and was cut in two. He was brought back to Saskatoon and Alvin and Alec and Myron were pallbearers at his funeral.

Most of the time Alvin was depressed and angry. Martha tried to boost his spirits by telling him that there were good times and bad times and that when they were this bad they always got better. Only to Martha would Alvin read his poems and talk about the things he wanted to do. And she would say, "And you will do them, too. Just you wait and see." She was sure that, with God's help, Alvin would some day be a great poet and make them all proud.

Alvin went to the library and brought home books by Proust and Shaw and Eugene O'Neill and Kierkegaard and Dostoevsky. Martha read the books, too, and they would discuss them endlessly.

When the phoney war was over and recruiting was high, Myron joined the navy, took officers' training, and was given command of a corvette on the North Atlantic. He finished the war as a commander and stayed with the navy. As happened with many other young men who'd been unemployed and apparently useless during the Depression, the war gave him a chance to show his stuff and develop skills that he didn't know he had.

Things improved for the Windmar family, too. Will got a job in a wartime office. Olive had finished high school and got a job as a clerk in the lingerie department at Eaton's. Gwen went to university, the beginning of her long, distinguished scholastic career. The war was good for everybody.

Alvin got a job with the CNR as an express porter and was paid by the hour to load cream cans and quarters of beef into express cars. But when the Germans overran most of Europe in the summer of 1940, there was a great need for recruits. Alec had an idea.

"We join the reserves, see, and then they can't draft us. Home defence, that's the thing."

So he and Alvin went down to the old armouries, just over the bridge, and enlisted in the Saskatoon Light Infantry. They were issued uniforms and greatcoats and boots and once a week they would take drill and training in the big barn-like armouries. Alvin hated it all. Not the route marches – he'd always liked walking – but he detested being shouted at and roundly cursed by sergeants and officers.

He suffered every kind of humilation since leaving school, and this was the worst of all. Why did they have to be so goddamned miserable and mean, he'wondered. And then he realized that often when you give a man authority he immediately becomes miserable and mean.

Worst of all was the bayonet drill. They were ordered to run up to a dummy and shove the bayonet through its guts. "An upward thrust, lads. Enter just below the ribs and then upward to the heart. Then give it a twist and pull it out and be ready for the next Nazi son of a bitch. Just remember, he'd bayonet your baby brother and rape your sister." All of this was to be accompanied by a blood-curdling yell, which Alvin never mastered.

And they soon found out that they weren't getting all this training to fight on the home front. They were expected to "go active." Each evening, at the conclusion of the drill, the major, an insurance agent in civilian life, would sit them down on the floor and lecture them about the need for men and tell them how he knew none of them wanted to be "yellow bellies" who shirked their duty to King and Country.

Then they were lined up and told that anyone who wanted to volunteer should take five paces forward, about-turn, and face the yellow bellies who hadn't volunteered. Many men who never intended to found themselves taking those five paces forward, but not Alvin.

And then he met Samantha and fell in love.

Alvin had never loved anyone before, except Martha. Certainly not his brothers and sisters. Them he put up with. He had always been a loner; he hid his feelings or expressed them in poetry. He was, as his sister Olive said, a sitting duck for any smart cookie who took a liking to him.

He met Samantha at a dance in the Cave, where Art Silvers and His Silvery Seven played on weekends. It was the first dance he'd been to since high school and Alec had talked him into going. "Now that we've got some money, let's have some fun."

It was fate, the way he met her. She'd had an argument

with her escort, who wanted her to go out into the parking lot and have a snort from his crock of rye. When she refused he went alone, and Samantha looked around for somebody with whom she could "show him a thing or two."

She spotted Alvin. He was standing alone, absent-mindedly watching the dancers. She went up to him.

"Hello. Would you care to dance?" she said.

He focused on her then and saw a tall girl with long black hair and a glowing complexion. She had a magnificent figure and a large, generous mouth and the loveliest eyes he'd ever looked into.

"Where did you come from?" he asked.

"What do you mean?"

"Oh, I know you. You're Norma Shearer. But what are you doing here?"

Her laugh was low and throaty.

"Well?"

He took her in his arms and that was it. When the song was over, he held on to her until the next one started.

When her date came back in, smelling of cheap rye, they were still dancing. He came up to them and tapped Alvin on the shoulder.

"That's my girl you've got there."

"Away, slight man." Alvin kept on dancing. He was a good dancer and so was Samantha. The toothy youth followed them.

"What the hell? That's my girl!"

"Then why did you leave her alone?"

"None of your damned business."

"If she were my girl, I'd never flee from her side." Alvin was in a heady mood. "Matter of fact, I don't think I ever will."

"Oh yeah? Maybe you'd like to step out into the alley?"

"Nope."

"Well, Jesus Christ, this is the damnedest thing I ever saw!"

"Suppose we ask the lady. After all, she is a lady, not a girl, and unless I'm mistaken she's not anyone's property."

Samantha stepped back - Alvin had been holding her tightly through this exchange - and said, "Herb, why don't you go out and have another drink? This gentleman will take me home."

The youth sized Alvin up, swore again, and marched off. Alvin was glad he did. He wasn't a fighter. In fact, he wasn't sure but what he might be a coward. But he was sure he would have fought for this woman. Now he felt big and expansive and fine. At the end of the dance he called a taxi and she gave the driver her address. Before she got out of the taxi, she kissed Alvin thoroughly on the mouth and asked him to call her; then she ran into the house.

"Where to now?" the taxi driver asked.

"The moon, by way of the Big Dipper and all the heavenly bodies. I'll walk."

He paid for the taxi and walked home, singing "You Were Meant for Me" and occasionally running a few steps.

When he got home Martha was still up, reading in the living room.

"Hi, honey bunch," Alvin shouted. "I'm in love!"

She didn't say anything corny. Just, "Want to tell me about it?"

"Yep. Her name is Samantha and she walks in beauty."

Martha took his hand and said simply, "I'm glad."

Alvin's life changed then. From being a lonely, frustrated, petulant, aloof youth he was transformed into a happy, funny, cheerful man.

He continued to work for the CNR and whenever he had time he took Samantha dancing or to a movie or driving in Tom's car, which Tom generously loaned with the admonition, "Don't do anything I wouldn't do."

They would park on the river bank near the university and pet. She was so ardent it frightened him, and something held him back. Perhaps it was fear that he wouldn't be able to perform; perhaps it was caution brought about by all the lectures he'd had from teachers and at Sunday school about the horrors of venereal disease; or his uncertain future; or a combination of all three. In any case he never did, as Tom would say, "slip it into her."

And she seemed to appreciate it. "You have to protect me from myself," she would say, and Alvin had some idea that he was being noble.

And then he met her family. George Romley was the president and owner of a large wholesale food business. Since people had to eat, the Depression hadn't affected him too much, and now, with the government buying tons of food for the troops, he was doing very well indeed.

Their house, on Idylwild Avenue, was big and brick and surrounded by lawns and shrubs. Alvin's first meal with them was an ordeal. Although his parents had been poor since he was eleven, Martha had always maintained correct decorum at meals and Alvin's manners were impeccable. No, it was George. He'd been a major in the First World War and had won military honours. His one regret was that he had no son to carry on the military tradition.

"What branch of the service are you planning to enter?" he asked Alvin.

"Well, right now I'm in the SLI Reserves."

"Excellent. Excellent. You'll be getting your chance to go active any day, I suppose. Ah, I wish I were thirty years younger. Canada has always supported the Mother Country in her hours of need and she will again. If that nincompoop of a Mackenzie King just had more backbone. Afraid of Quebec, that's the trouble. Him and his zombies."

"What's a zombie?" his wife asked him. She was a plump, pleasant matron, much younger than her husband. She had taken the trouble to ascertain that Alvin came from a good family even if they had been hard hit by the Depression.

"A zombie is slang for the young, healthy men who won't volunteer for active service. Who hide behind King's ridiculous policy of no conscription."

Alvin was looking at Samantha when her father said this, and he wondered how he was ever going to confess to her that he was a zombie. She was glowing with pride and patriotism and bravery and all those other things that caused many a young man to rally to the flag.

And so it came about that the next time volunteers were ordered to take five paces forward and about-turn, Alvin was with them. He tried to avoid Alec's eyes, which were filled with surprise and contempt, but he couldn't quite make it. When the parade had been dismissed, the two friends walked out the armouries door together and stopped.

"What the hell got into you?" Alec demanded.

"Well. . . ."

"It's that damned broad you've been seeing. That's it, isn't it?"

"Not exactly."

"What the hell do you mean? You've been bending my ear with all that pacifist talk about what do we owe a country that couldn't even provide a job and how the war is arranged by the munitions manufacturers - and now you go bloody active!"

"It's just, well - "

"It's just that twitchy little cunt!"

Alvin hit him then. He had never hit anyone in his life and abhorred physical violence. And Alec hit back. It wasn't much of a fistfight. An officer came along and broke it up and then said something to Alvin that made him ashamed and furious.

"Don't worry about those yellow bellies. You'll soon be far away from them."

But when he told Samantha what he had done she was so warm and loving and proud that Alvin gained confidence and took the initiative in making love to her. And once started he was like a starving man who came to the feast. Every time they met until he was shipped out they made love, in the car, on the grass of the river bank, in her bed when her parents were out. And when he left her she clung to him and wept and called him her hero and vowed to be true. For Alvin there was no doubt that Samantha was his one and only woman.

Alvin's first camp was at Dundurn, about thirty miles south of Saskatoon, and in the most barren, hot, dusty, uninspiring part of the province. With the other recruits he marched, ran, rode in machine-gun carriers, and dodged live bullets among the sand dunes.

But Dundurn was close enough to Saskatoon for him to see his love occasionally. Still overwhelmed with the euphoria of love, he applied himself as best he could and, although he had absolutely no aptitude for soldiering, managed to learn a thing or two about it.

Then they were shipped to Petawawa, in Ontario, which was a bit of an adventure since he had never before been east of Saskatchewan. He wrote to Samantha every night, letters filled with humour, puckishness, poetry, and adoration. And she wrote back letters that, had he been in a less dream-like state, he would have recognized as trite and dull.

And so it went until he was shipped to England and began intensive training there. He continued to write regularly, but Samantha's letters were less frequent and loving. Then came the inevitable "Dear John," in which she informed him that she was about to be married to a friend of the family and that she hoped it wouldn't break his heart. "You'll probably find some nice English girl and fall in love again," she said, not realizing how thoroughly heartless and brutal she was being.

As for Alvin, he reverted to his old confused, frustrated, disillusioned, unhappy self. His soldiering deteriorated to a hopeless mess. His sergeant and the lieutenant in charge of his platoon knew what had happened to him and made some allowances.

He went to London on leave with a chum, got lost in the blackout, and got hopelessly drunk. He was picked up by a bobby, at whom he swore in the best Saskatchewanese. The MPs got hold of him and he was returned to camp to be punished.

Then he became reckless. He volunteered for every dangerous assignment and was almost killed several times. When it came time for volunteers for the Dieppe raid, he was the first to step forward. The special commando training he received served to dull the pain in his head, and when his platoon was landed on the beach during that cruel, hopeless exercise, he had barely taken two paces up the beach when a bullet hit him squarely in the forehead and ended his suffering for good. He lay there alone, as he always had been. The tide washed his body out into the channel, and it was never recovered. "Missing and presumed dead."

The girl who had inspired him to become a soldier cried a little when she heard of his death, and then went off to a dance at the country club.

The effect on the Windmar family was traumatic. None of them was quite the same again. Somehow Alvin came to represent the epitome of hard luck. He had never had anything else. His whole life had been a slogging tramp across a barren wasteland with only the tiny oasis of Samantha near the end, and she had turned out to be a cruel mirage.

Will, whose natural optimism had somehow managed to transcend his own bouts of hard luck, found it hard to cope with Alvin's. "If only he had survived that rotten war and had some of the good times that followed. I never should have let him enlist," he would say, forgetting that he had nothing to do with it and couldn't have prevented it if he'd tried.

Tom reacted with anger and a touch of guilt. He had survived the war by ignoring it. Since he was married with three kids, his name never came up for the draft. He was wont to allude to Alvin as "that poor little bugger." (He had first used the phrase of endearment one time Alvin was lost in the hayfield.) "Come to think of it, he'd have been better off if he had got a leg cut off that day."

Olive took out her anger on Samantha. "Every time I see that brat it makes my blood boil! Sashaying around the country club!"

Gwen's analysis was detached and analytical. "We can't blame Samantha," she explained. "She acted according to her personality. It wasn't her fault if Alvin read into her character more than was really there. It's a common reaction of people in love. Which accounts for numerous divorces."

To which Olive replied, "Never mind that psychological shit. Alvin is dead, for Christ's sake!"

But it was Martha who suffered most. Alvin's death left a hole in her life that nothing could fill. She kept his picture on her dresser, one of the few pictures in which he was smiling; she kept all his letters. She meticulously collected all his poems and paid a local printer to print and bind them into a thin volume. On the cover she pasted one of her pictures of Alvin.

Now as she lay dying in the big upstairs bedroom that faced the river, where Alvin had so often played, her thoughts were of her lost boy. Now and then she would mutter, "There, there, don't cry."

To Gwen, who had talked and lectured and written about death but who had never before sat and held the hand of a dying woman, Martha's illness opened up a line of thought.

"Perhaps this is what immortality is," she explained. "They say that we meet our loved ones after death. Well, if our last thoughts are about them, that is what we carry into eternity. If our last thoughts are filled with hate, then that is surely hell."

Chapter Fifteen

We get what we deserve in this life, Hugh mused as Tom's car purred along the highway towards Harman. We make our choices and we live by them. A man is all kinds of a fool if he whines about the outcome.

One way or another he had expressed this sentiment a dozen times in his writing. Then why was he feeling so blue, thinking about Elaine? What would his life have been like if he hadn't abandoned her? The love he never again knew, the children and the grandchildren he never had. Well, didn't the fact that he never had them prove he'd never really wanted them?

He hadn't written to Elaine to tell her where he was. And he never found out what happened to her after he left. Perhaps he would find out now.

He couldn't get Galsworthy's story "The Apple Tree" out of his mind. It is a story of a city fellow who has an affair with a simple country girl. And when he leaves her, pregnant, she kills herself and is buried at the crossroads. God. Elaine wouldn't do that, surely. Well, he rationalized, there really had been nothing worth writing about.

He remembered that train ride east. Leaving the hot, dusty prairie just east of Winnipeg and entering the land of the spruce forests and lakes. He had gone from southern Manitoba to northern Ontario without changing direction. He had never seen forests, and the Saskatchewan River was the largest body of water he'd seen. And the rock. As a teacher he'd known the geography of Canada quite well. The Canadian Shield he thought he knew all about, but he knew nothing about it. He half-wished he had some of his brighter students with him to see it.

The strangest part was that he felt not like someone leaving home but like someone coming home. The trees and the streams and the rock were like old friends. He could see only fifty feet or so on either side of the track, but it didn't seem to bother him. Could trees and streams be in his genes?

And when they left the shield at the Severn River and got into the rolling farmland of southern Ontario, with the strange garden-sized fields, some even surrounded by rail fences, and the huge unpainted barns and silos, he felt even more at home. This was his father's country and his grandfather's and his great-grandfather's. The flat, endless prairie he'd known since birth was the unusual landscape. This, like the fields and hills of Ireland, was the natural landscape. As the train passed through stands of hardwood, maple, elm, oak, and hemlock, all trees he'd never seen before, he was delighted. And then, late on a Sunday afternoon, Lake Ontario, and finally Toronto.

The train roared past factories and warehouses such as he had never seen. And familiar names. Neilson Chocolate. Gooderham and Worts, Massey-Harris. This was where these things came from. And finally into the long tunnel of Union Station, and he was there.

He followed the crowd through passageways and up marble stairs, through the big cathedral-like foyer and out onto Front Street, with the Royal York Hotel blocking out everything else. By God, he would sleep there one night at least. And so he carried his bags across the street, surrendered them to a doorman, and registered.

"I'd like a window facing the lake, if possible," he said to the clerk.

"I think we have one."

In his room he stood before the window and looked out over Union Station at the lake and Toronto Island. The ferry was halfway across the harbour and small sailboats skittered around it. Toronto, the land of his imaginings,

Toronto the good, Toronto the stuffy, Toronto the city with some history. Old Fort York, Muddy York. Most of all, Toronto the home of publishers, producers, people who would pay money for writing.

There, on a stand beside the bed, was a telephone and on a shelf an enormous telephone book. He lifted the heavy book to the bed and began to look up numbers. Moor, H. Napier. By God, he was in the book. Hugh could call him on the phone. B.K. Sandwell was there, too. And Morley Callaghan. They all lived in this city. Tomorrow he would look for a boarding house and then perhaps he might call them.

After a shower (he had never had one before) he went out onto Front Street and walked along to Yonge. Famous Yonge Street. He walked north to King Street and there, halfway along the block, was the Bank of Commerce building, highest building in the British Empire. Across the street was the *Toronto Star*. He bought a *Star* from a newsie for three cents and tucked it under his arm, like any real Torontonian, and proceeded north on Yonge Street. He was surprised that nothing was open, not a restaurant or a coffee shop, and hardly anyone was on the street. Sunday night to be sure, but Toronto?

He paused in front of Loews Theatre and looked at the movie posters. *A Day at the Races* with the Marx Brothers. Well, he would have to see that.

A small man came and stood beside him. A dirty-looking little man who badly needed a haircut and a shave and smelled of cheap wine.

"Evening, mate," the man said.

"Good evening." His first Toronto contact.

"Looks like a good movie."

"Yes, it does."

"I wonder if you could help me out, mate. You see, my ship sailed without me. The *William G. Hardy* she was, from England. Well, I tell you, mate, I don't mind admitting I took a few too many when I came ashore and then I got rolled and everything taken, wallet, papers, everything."

Hugh knew this was a line, but he didn't quite know how to stop it.

"If I just had a couple of bucks, I could get to a friend's house, lives in a town just north of here. It would be a big help to me, mate, if you could see your way clear to advance me that much."

"Well. . . ."

"You give me your name and address and I'll pay you back, I swear to God I will, mate. I haven't eaten in two days and I got no place to sleep. A couple of bucks would solve my problem."

Hugh gave him a two-dollar bill and when the little man's face took on a cunning look and he began again, Hugh stopped him. "Listen, friend, take the two dollars and buy whatever you want with it, but leave me alone."

"I swear on my mother's grave."

"Leave your mother out of this. Your story is worth two dollars. Now beat it."

The look on the weasel face changed from cunning to hatred. "Listen, you damned bastard – " But just then a policeman rounded the corner and came towards them, and the little man vanished as quickly as he'd come.

Hugh went back to the hotel. He was hungry, but the restaurants in the hotel were closed. He asked the room clerk where he could get a sandwich.

"You registered here, sir?"

"Yes, room 602."

"Just give room service a call. They'll look after you."

Hugh didn't know if he should tip the man or not, but decided against it.

The next morning, Monday, it was raining. The first real rain Hugh had seen all year. It came pelting down on the sidewalk and the streets and pounded against the hotel window. He looked out on a grey, wet world. People were hurrying in and out of Union Station with umbrellas and climbing into taxis. A streetcar went past, not the kind they had in Saskatoon, which clanged and banged, but a streamlined streetcar that slid silently along the track like an automobile.

Well, the first things he would need were a raincoat and an umbrella. He had never owned either. On the floor below the lobby of the Royal York was a row of stores. He found what he needed, then paid for them. He realized he would have to start conserving his money.

First he would find a boarding house. A taxi driver might help. So he checked out of his beautiful room, and carrying his beat-up suitcase and wearing his new coat, he stood just inside the door of the hotel. The doorman whistled for a taxi and Hugh got in.

"Where to?" asked the driver.

"Well, I don't rightly know."

The driver turned in his seat. He was a man of indefinite age, somewhere between thirty and sixty, with a weather-beaten face.

"Just got in from the west, eh?"

"How do you know?"

"I can tell. I got a sister in Regina. Jeez, what a country. Freeze the balls off a brass monkey. You lookin' for a place to stay?"

"Well."

"Listen. For Chrissake, all you guys are the same. Got some idea Toronto cabbies are going to rook you. Take you miles out of your way. All bullshit."

"Okay. I'll need a boarding house."

"Cheap, too, eh? Well, listen. Church Street or Jarvis are where most of them are. Jarvis is a little gamier. Church ain't bad. You can walk to most of the newspapers from there."

"What makes you think I'm interested in newspapers?"

"Well, ain't you?"

"Matter of fact, yes."

"I can tell. Okay, I'll take you over to Church. Someplace just south of Carlton, that ain't bad."

"Is that near College Street?"

"That is College Street. Changes its name at Yonge."

He started the car and slid into the traffic, barely missing another taxi, made a right turn onto York, and went north to Adelaide. Hugh was amazed at the way he manoeuvred through the traffic and took the corners. Adelaide took him over to Church, where he turned left and slowed down, looking at the large brick houses set close to the street.

"Sure are a lot of brick houses!" Hugh said.

"All of 'em. City regulation. Can't build a frame house in Toronto."

"In the province of forests you can't build a frame house? Out in Saskatchewan, where there are no lumber trees, all the houses are frame."

"Conspiracy of the railroads. Here's one."

He pulled to the curb and stopped in front of an ancient three-storey, grey-brick house in a row of similar houses. A sign in the window said ROOM FOR RENT.

"Want me to wait?" the taxi driver asked as he lifted Hugh's suitcase and portable typewriter from the seat beside him.

"No. This looks as good as any." He paid the driver and thanked him and carried his things up the front steps and rang the bell. A middle-aged woman with her black hair in curlers answered the door.

"You have a room?"

"That's what the sign says." She was looking him over carefully. "Ten dollars a week. No women. No visitors after eleven."

"May I see it?"

She led the way up the stairs and then up another flight and opened the door to an attic room. Two small windows looked out on the street. There was a bed and a dresser and a straight chair.

"Bathroom's on the floor below."

The room was clean and smelled all right.

"Where you from?" the lady asked.

"Saskatchewan."

"Is that anywhere near Regina?"

"Yeah. Quite close."

"I got a cousin in Regina. Cold out there."

"Indeed it is."

"You got a job?"

"Not yet, but I hope to soon."

"I'll need the rent in advance. Not that I don't trust you, you understand, just a rule."

Hugh gave her a ten-dollar bill and she left. He sat down on the bed and peered through the dirty windows at the dirty sky, still pouring rain. He felt unutterably depressed. The phrase "A stranger in a strange land" kept running through his mind. A schoolteacher from a tiny hamlet in Saskatchewan.

He decided he couldn't go out job hunting in the rain. He opened his Remington portable and set it on the bed, rolled in some paper, pulled the chair up to the bed, and began to type a description of his trip and his impressions of Ontario. He tied it to the stories Will had told, for Will had boarded not far from this room, maybe even in the same house.

It was a good angle, he decided, and the piece went well. He told about his fears of big-city slickers and the helpful taxi driver and when he finished he had about fifteen hundred words. Always a careful typist, his work needed little revision. He put the story into a cardboard folder with a sigh of satisfaction.

Then he put on his raincoat, took his umbrella, and sallied forth. He found a restaurant on the corner of Carlton and Jarvis and for thirty-five cents got a decent meal of liver and onions.

When he was paying, he asked the counterman the best way to get to the *Toronto Star*.

"Just grab the streetcar at the corner, transfer at Yonge – that's just a block – go south to King and walk half a block west."

So the next morning he took the streetcar, one of the fast, smooth, one-operator jobs, and arrived at the *Toronto Star* building. He entered the high, marble-walled foyer and faced four elevators. He asked the operator for the editorial department and was let off at the third floor in a huge room filled with desks and chairs and telephones, working reporters, and the clatter of typewriters.

He spotted a desk with a sign that said INFORMATION and asked the girl if he could see the editor.

"Mr. Hindmarsh is busy just now. What do you want to see him about?"

"I want to sell him a story."

"Oh, I see. Well, you just leave it with me, along with your name and phone number and – "

"I don't want to leave it. I want to see the editor."

"But that isn't the way it's done. You leave your manuscript with me and – "

"No."

"Now see here. . . ."

Just then a stoutish man in shirt sleeves came by. He stopped and said, "What's the trouble, Mary?"

She sighed. "This gentleman insists on seeing the editor. I told him to leave his manuscript, but. . . ."

The stout man was looking at Hugh with a slight smile on his face. "What have you got?"

"I want to see the editor."

"I'm the features editor." He held out his hand and Hugh gave him the manuscript. The man looked at it carefully. Hugh was sure nobody could read anything that fast. "Just got into town from Saskatchewan, eh?"

"Yeah. That's – "

"I know where it is. This isn't bad. I think we could spot it on Saturday's feature page."

"You could? But you hardly glanced at it."

"I read it. Can't pay you much. Twenty-five okay?"

"Yeah, sure."

"And look. We need stuff from the west. Just how bad it is out there. Maybe you could do a round-up piece for us. You know, dust and grasshoppers and so on. Where did you live?"

"I was teaching in a town called Harman."

"Teaching. Even better. I hear some teachers aren't getting any pay at all."

"That's right."

"Okay. Give us about two thousand words. And be specific. Real examples with names. How soon can you do it?"

"Right away."

"Okay. Bring it directly to me. That office over there." He scribbled a note on a pad. "Give this to the cashier over there and get your twenty-five."

"This is easy. This is a cup of tea. Nothing to it," Hugh muttered to himself as he walked up Yonge Street. "If I'd known it was going to be this easy, I'd have been here long ago." The traffic on Yonge Street played a symphony of satisfaction.

When he got back to his boarding house he asked the landlady for a little table he could use for his typewriter.

"Well, I really don't have - "

"You see, I just sold a story to the *Toronto Star* and they want another."

"You did?" She was obviously sceptical.

He took the cheque from his pocket and showed it to her. She was impressed.

"Well, I think I can find something."

And she did. An old walnut washstand from the basement. Right height, but no place for his feet. He put the typewriter on top and a leg on each side and it worked fine. When he got into the story he realized there was too much to tell. And so he wrote the story of Alvin's friend dying of peritonitis in a lonely farmhouse, and managed to work into the story a great deal about dust and grasshoppers and shrivelled crops. The editor liked it and paid him fifty dollars.

So with these two credits and his *Liberty* story, he began doing the rounds of magazines. He went to *Liberty* first. The editor, a tall, friendly man, explained that all the fiction came from the American branch of the magazine and he was responsible for non-fiction articles. But he had plenty of experienced writers to supply those. It was the same story at *Maclean's* and the *Canadian Home Journal* and *Saturday Night*. All the editors were friendly and helpful, but there were no assignments. So he went back to the *Star*, but they had two good pieces about the prairies and weren't buying any more.

Then came the really tough part, trying to make enough money to eat and pay his rent. There were few jobs of any kind and plenty of unemployed people. He tried selling vacuum cleaners door to door and then encyclopaedias, and developed a new respect for anyone who could make money that way. He washed dishes in a restaurant and worked in a car wash. And all the time he kept writing, short stories, radio plays, humour pieces, but nothing sold.

When the summer heat finally dissipated and the beautiful Ontario autumn arrived, he felt his spirits rise again. The many-coloured leaves of the immense oaks and maples in the parks and along the boulevards delighted him.

One day he walked up to Bloor Street and crossed the bridge that led to Rosedale. The colour was even more beautiful. He saw wide lawns, immense trees, and fine brick homes. He found his way through the maze of streets and finally arrived at the house where Martha had lived as a child, although his grandparents no longer lived there. He stood in front of the house and thought of her life, and for the first time realized how traumatic it must have been for her to move from this place to the prairies. And all the years between seemed to dissolve, for the house looked exactly like the pictures Martha had shown him. Even the maples in the front yard were the same. It gave him a peculiar sense of going back in time.

Hugh walked back to his rooming house on Church Street, climbed the stairs to his little room, sat on the bed, and decided that, come what may, he wasn't going back to Saskatchewan.

Then came the Toronto winter, wet and windy and cold. The little room that had been so unbearably hot during the summer was frigid; the heat from the small, balky furnace somehow got lost in the maze of rusty ducts between basement and attic. His bank account was dwindling: in four months he hadn't sold a line of writing. He was trying to write half-hour radio plays for the series *Curtain Time*. He came close, but no cigar, and all the time he was learning.

By spring he was just about broke. He paid his rent, but he was living mostly on nuts and raisins and day-old bread, which he ate in his room. He was beginning to think of chucking it and going back to Saskatoon when he met Melba.

She moved into the other attic room and he encountered her as he was going down the stairs. She was dark-haired with wide-apart dark eyes, a beautiful complexion, and an air of energy, drive, and intelligence. Hugh stood and stared.

"Hello," she said easily. "You must be Hugh."

"Yes. How did you know?"

"And you are a writer, but you haven't sold anything in months. Mrs. Lack told me all about you. Do you like wine?"

"Why, yes."

"I have a bottle. Just got it from the liquor store. Will you join me?"

"Of course. It's very kind of you."

"You're very polite. Are all people from Saskatchewan so polite?"

He laughed. "Not by a damned sight. Before I came here I was a school principal. It's hard to shake."

"You? A principal? You look more like a student." She led the way into her room, which was the same as his only different. A woman's room with a woman's touches.

"You know all about me. How about you?"

"I'm from London, Ontario, the stuffiest city in the world, and I've come to Toronto to make it big. And I shall."

"I believe you." He sipped his wine. "And in the meantime?"

"Waitress in the King Edward Hotel dining room. The tips aren't as big as in some other places, but they'll do. And when the war starts – "

"What war?"

"Where have you been? You must read. You must listen to the radio. You must know what that swine Hitler is doing, especially to the Jews! I'm Jewish." She sighed. "I can see that makes no difference to you."

"Should it?"

"No. But to too many people it does. Are you hungry?"

"Do I look hungry?"

"Yeah." She produced a plate of Danish pastry and chocolate eclairs. "From the restaurant. They're a day old, so they give them to us. I eat like a pig at that restaurant."

"You don't show it!"

"Metabolism. Never put on weight. Besides, I run it off. When I'm not waitressing, I haunt the CBC. There are jobs for women there and I'm going to get one."

"I think you will."

"I like you, Hugh."

"You just met me."

"I can tell. You respect women. You don't say stupid things and you don't make passes."

"I shall one day."

"I hope so. But you have some manners, some finesse. My guess is you come from a good family."

"The best."

"I have a friend who buys writing. Works for an ad agency that produces a series of radio plays for kids. All about a wonder dog."

"I've heard of it. 'Prince, the Wonder Dog.' "

"That's the one. His writers are always quitting because of the lousy pay. Ever write for radio?"

"Constantly."

"Ever sold anything?"

"No."

"You could write this stuff. He needs a twelve-minute script every day and he pays ten dollars a script."

"Ten dollars?"

"Not much, but as much as you'll get. And listen, when you meet this guy, don't admit you've never sold any radio scripts. Whatever he wants, say you can do it."

"Okay, lead on."

Oscar Trap worked out of a small office in an old building. Next to the office he'd rigged up a studio for taping the shows. He was a middle-aged, plump man with a nervous tic. He looked at Hugh shrewdly.

"Ever write radio before?" Trap asked.

"Yep."

"Who for?"

"Radio station out west. Worked on a series of farm stories for a creamery."

"Oh. Well, this pays eight bucks a script."

"I was told it was ten."

"You could work up to ten." He pawed around in a drawer. "Here's an outline of what we do. Never more than three characters, get it?"

"Yep."

"The dog always the hero, always does something wonderful. That's why he's called the Wonder Dog. You can use lots of barking. We've got a good barker. That's the beauty of radio. We don't need a dog, wonderful or dumb. And remember, it's for kids. Ever write for kids?"

"Lots."

"Okay, let's see what you can do."

After a few tries, Hugh found writing the radio series comparatively easy. He'd always had dogs as a kid – Martha loved animals – and he found himself incorporating their whacky characters into the scripts. In due time he took over the series as other writers quit or went on to better things.

All through the hot, muggy summer of 1938, when Europe was getting ready to blow itself apart, he wrote about dogs. Soon he was able to finish his scripts by ten in the morning, which left him the rest of the day to do his own writing. In the evenings he and Melba found places to eat and drink, and they talked endlessly with the bright young people Melba attracted.

And so they became lovers. Neither wanted any kind of

permanent attachment. Both were too ambitious. Melba was good for Hugh. She had a strong, determined, aggressive personality and she knew what she wanted and where she was going. At the same time she was affectionate and sensitive. He had never known a person quite like her, and it made him realize the big difference between Saskatchewan and Toronto. Writers came to Toronto; Saskatchewan was where they left. From Melba he gained self-confidence and self-respect, just when he needed them most.

Then, on September 3, 1939, everything changed. Suddenly a country that had been comatose for ten years came to life. Young men who had little or no purpose in life, who were overwhelmed with poverty and boredom, saw a chance to change their lives. They joined the armed forces. By the thousands they turned up at the recruiting station in the CNE grounds, where they were inspected like beef, prodded, peered into, and stamped A-1 or rejected.

Others with more imagination held off. "If they want me they can come and get me" was their attitude. Hugh, always a pragmatist and an opportunist, was one of these. He stood on the corner of Yonge and Bloor and watched the young men dressed in navy blue or air-force khaki or army drab march past with bands playing and the words of Falstaff went through his mind: "Who hath honour, he who died a Tuesday."

And then he began to get phone calls from some of the editors at the newspapers. He went to see the editor at the *Star*, who said, "We can use you, but how long will you stay?"

"For as long as you want me."

"Four-F?"

"Yep. Bum right ear. Kid threw a rock at me when I was eight and busted the ear-drum." It had been George Yancy who'd done that when he and Hugh had been fighting over some marbles.

"Lucky for you," the editor said.

Hugh fixed him with a deadpan stare, which was to become his trademark. "Well, one's got to have some luck in this crazy world. Take you, now, you'll probably join Conn Smythe's battery and become a hero."

It wasn't the only job he was offered. "Six months ago nobody wanted me," he told Melba. "Now everybody wants me."

Melba got a position with the film section of the Wartime Information Bureau and went off to Ottawa. It was just the break she'd been waiting for, and it was the beginning of a great career in the film industry. She and Hugh got drunk together the night before she left and made glorious love on her brass bed. Both knew this was the end of their relationship and both were considerably relieved. After the war they met now and then, but both were climbing the ladder of success and the old fire was never rekindled.

When he learned of Alvin's death, Hugh cried.

When the war ended Hugh found himself in the right place at the right time. Everybody wanted writers. He dropped the newspaper and magazine work and concentrated on the CBC drama department. There were good directors and some of the best actors to be found anywhere. John Drainie, Tommy Tweed, Bernie Braden. Besides the CBC, there were commercial series, like Ford Theatre and Buckingham Theatre. Hugh worked feverishly and learned the craft of play-writing while getting paid for it. And all the time he was working on stage plays.

Because of his own good luck, he developed the philosophy that somewhere, sometime, everybody gets his chance. The important thing is to be able to take advantage of the opportunity when it comes.

And now it was 1980 and the world was getting ready to blow up again. This time, he knew, the blow-up would be bigger and more devastating. Hugh found the prospect ironical, but not too worrisome. He'd always known the world was a crazy place, filled with crazy people led by crazier people. Complete destruction seemed to him the logical final act of the farce.

Chapter Sixteen

It was all different. As he approached Harman, Hugh couldn't find any of the old landmarks. Wilson's farm with the big barn, the big slough near the road. And then, over to his left, he saw the elevators. He realized that the new highway by-passed the town.

He came to a little-used rutted road and thought it might lead into the town. After about a mile he crossed the tracks, and then he remembered. The tracks he and Elaine had walked along in the spring of 1937. Yeah, the only decent place to walk during the spring thaw, when the roads were quagmires of mud. Walking along those tracks in the spring sunshine, watching the gophers emerge and scamper across the partially snow-covered fields and then sit bolt upright before diving into their holes. And the crows winging overhead, cawing that first welcome sound of spring. And the blackbirds on the bulrushes that were beginning to turn green in the ditches along the track. Ducks flying overhead.

Spring on the prairies after the long, cold winter. Everything came to life. The purple crocuses on the bare knolls where the snow melted first. The horses turned out of the barn kicking up their heels with sheer joy, calves running around for the sake of running. Dogs following bitches, roosters chasing hens.

And the people. Shut up all winter, too, and in those days with no fresh vegetables or fruit. Sitting on the sunny side of their houses, soaking up the warmth. Kids in the school yard playing marbles and skipping and chasing each other. Older boys playing catch in the sun. Senior girls walking together talking, absorbing sunlight.

And young men's fancies definitely did turn to thoughts of love.

The school had been on this road, which ran along the outskirts of the town. And there it was, surrounded by weeds, the baseball diamond completely obliterated by them, a couple of posts and some ragged wire mesh where the backstop had been. No sign of the basketball court.

And the school itself, unpainted and neglected, windows all boarded up. He drove through the familiar gate and stopped near the door. A hand-lettered sign said KEEP OUT.

He sat and stared at the doors. The years dropped away. So this was it. It really existed. Sometimes during those busy, eventful years he'd half-wondered if he dreamed the whole experience. And Elaine had sometimes seemed like a dream, too.

He got out of the car, went up the steps to the door, and tried the knob. To his surprise, the door creaked open. Inside was the dark hall with the bulletin board where he used to post the names of the teams for recess play. The last notice put up by whatever teacher was last there was still pinned to the board. It said, "Students will not run in the hall."

The three familiar rooms still where they should be. He went into the senior room. His desk and chair were still there. There were rows of empty seats, some broken, all covered with dust. And there was the desk where Elaine had sat, looking up at him with that amused, coquettish smile. A room full of ghosts.

He went back into the hall and closed the door softly behind him. All was silent. He remembered Alfred Noyes's poem "The Listeners." "Only a host of phantom listeners that dwelt in the lone house then." He tiptoed to the front door and out into the sunlight.

From there he stood looking over the town, but there was no town. At least not much. The hotel, the great three-storey hotel that had once stood above all the other buildings, where was it?

With a slight tightening in his gut, Hugh walked out

of the school yard and down to the corner. Then he followed the road that paralleled the railway tracks. The lumber yard was completely gone, only a patch of pigweed where it had been. He reached the corner where the station had been, but the station was gone. He turned down the main street. Rorie's store, once on the corner, was gone; Pop's restaurant was gone; the post office was gone. The town hall where he'd first danced with Elaine was no more. There were a few houses scattered across the prairie. He saw a fairly new house on the main street and when he reached it he saw a sign that said POST OFFICE.

He pushed open the door and entered a tiny room with a wicket and perhaps twenty-five post boxes built into the wall. He went to the wicket and rang a little hand bell. A man who appeared to be almost his own age appeared.

"Yes?" he asked. "What can I do for you?"

"Well, for one thing, you can tell me what's happened to the town."

"This town? Been like this for twenty years."

"What happened?"

"Well, they closed the school and the elevators and then the trains quit stopping. There wasn't much left." He peered closely at Hugh. "You ever live here?"

"Yes, many years ago."

The thin man peered more closely. "Teacher?"

"Principal of the school."

A big grin spead over the man's face, a grin that was familiar somehow. He shoved his hand through the wicket. "I thought so. Hugh Windmar, isn't it?"

"Why, yes." He took the hand. "And you?"

"Tod Sanderson. You came to the farm for supper. I was one of the little runts. Grade seven - let's see, no, six - when you were here."

"For God's sake. Tod Sanderson. Well, how are you?"

"As you can see. Government job. Got a bit banged up in the war."

"I see. This seems to be the only thing left in town."

"Yep. Harman's finished. Just gradually went downhill.

Then when the new highway by-passed us, that was the end."

"The hotel. What happened to it?"

"Burned down. Let me see, must be twenty years ago. Tom Whitaker hauled the town hall away to keep chickens in. How'd you get here, by car?"

"Yes, I left it over at the school."

Tod Sanderson laughed. A replica of his father's laugh. "The school. Some mess, eh? Closed it about ten years ago. All the kids go by bus to the school in Harris."

"Well, they'll get a better education, I suppose. Say, is there anybody left I might know? The Walpers?"

"Frank and Jenny left. Went to Saskatoon. They broke up soon after. Frank died of some kind of cancer. Remember how he could pitch ball?"

"I remember."

"Hey, where are my manners? Don't stand out there. Come in and have a cup of tea. Marjorie was one of your students, too." He disappeared from the wicket and opened the door beside it. "We sure are proud of all that great success you've had," he said, as Hugh went through the door into a pleasant living room.

Marjorie Sanderson was a plump, pleasant woman. She made tea. "The children here go to school on the bus now. They're gone from seven-thirty in the morning until five in the afternoon. I think it was better the way we had it, eh? Just walk across town to school and home for lunch."

"I guess they get a better education now," Tod said. "They have better equipment, libraries, gymnasiums, and all that stuff. I remember the teacher had to make half our chemistry equipment." He laughed his Sanderson laugh. "A Bunsen burner made of an old coal-oil lamp and callipers made from clothes hangers."

Hugh didn't want to talk about school. He wanted to find out about Elaine, but he couldn't bring up her name. "And your brother John? Where is he?"

"Dead. Killed in the invasion of France."

"Damn!"

"He didn't need to have gone, neither. Too old, really. I think he mostly wanted to get away from the old man. And then with Jean gone – "

"Jean McTavish? What happened to her?"

"She left. Tired of waiting for Johnnie, I guess. God damn that Depression. He did all the work around the farm, but there was no way he could get one of his own. And the old man, well. . . ." There was no grin on Tod's face now.

"What a waste."

Marjorie was looking at him quizzically. "You haven't asked about Elaine."

There it was. He felt his guts go weak.

"Yeah, you were pretty sweet on her as I remember," Tod said.

"Yes, yes, I was. What happened. I mean. . . ."

"Oh, Elaine's okay. Married a real nice guy."

"Not Leonard?"

"That goof? Gosh, no. Don't know what happened to him. No, fellow named Walter Godfrey. She lives on a big farm just east of town. Still as full of life as ever. Into everything. Still working for the NDP."

"Children?"

"Eight. Got a dozen grandchildren, and more to come."

Grandchildren. Of course. Everybody his age had grandchildren. Well, welcome to them.

"Say, she'd be tickled to death to see you."

"She would?"

"Sure thing. Follows your career pretty closely. You know, reviews in *Maclean's* and such. You're famous around here."

"Oh."

"I can give her a ring."

"On the phone?"

Again the laugh. "Oh, yeah, we got phones and a lot of other things we didn't have when you were here. Electricity, for instance."

"Yes, of course. I wasn't thinking. You had phones when I was here. Boy, did you have phones!"

"Yeah, Maggie Jones in the phone office knew all about

everybody's business. Didn't need a newspaper, with that party line. It's better now. Want me to call?"

There was something in Tod's voice that sounded like a challenge. "She may not be home, always driving around the country to some meeting or other. She's a big wheel in the NDP. Member of the provincial house for a term."

"Good for her." He felt he should say something more, but what?

Tod got up and went over to a white phone that sat on a small table and dialled a number. Hugh waited. Damn, why did he feel like a patient waiting to see the dentist? Tod listened. "One ring." He counted up to eight. "Nobody home."

"Her husband?"

"Dead. Heart attack six months ago. They were getting ready for a trip to the old country. Shame, after working so hard all those years."

"And Elaine still lives there?"

"Yeah. Rents the farm to a neighbour, but still lives in the big house. Says she wants a place where the kids can come to visit. They do, too. Say, why don't you have lunch with us? Then we'll try her again."

But Hugh had found out what he'd wanted to know. All these years he'd wondered about her, worried about her. What had happened when he left her? Deserted her, abandoned her, when she was pregnant and helpless.

He stood up. "Thanks very much, Tod. But I want to run up to Harris and look up some old friends. I'll be back this way and I'll look her up then." But he had no intention of coming this way again, ever. All he wanted was to get away from this place forever.

Before Tod could answer, he heard a door open at the back of the house.

"Yoohoo, anybody home?" The same voice, the same lilt.

"In here!" Marjorie got up and hurried into the kitchen.

"I brought some stuff from the garden," the voice continued. "It's growing that fast I can't keep up with it." She stopped at the living-room door and stared. Then, as naturally as if they'd seen each other only yesterday, "Hughie? Is it really you?"

She hadn't changed much, still trim and smart-looking. The brown hair had gone grey and she had a few wrinkles, but they were laugh wrinkles. Much the same sparkle in her eye.

"Yes, Elaine, it's really me." He fought for composure. "It's, uh, good to see you."

"And you."

"I hear great things about you. Oh hell, that sounds pretentious."

"It sure does." Her laugh rang out.

Tod stood up. "Marjorie, I've got to go down the street and see a man about a dog. Come with me."

"What? Oh, yes, of course. You will excuse us, I'm sure." She took her husband's arm and they went out the back.

"What about the post office?" Hugh asked, and then wished he hadn't.

"Nobody comes in until the truck brings the mail at four o'clock," Elaine said. "I'm sure they'll be back by then."

"He's a, uh, nice man," Hugh said, as they chose chairs across the room from each other.

"Yes, it's amazing how well they all got on when I just up and left them."

"When was that?"

"Right after you went away. I met Walter at a dance, and. . . ."

He realized she didn't know he'd heard of her pregnancy, and he wasn't about to tell her.

"And your own children?"

"All left the nest. The oldest boy, who always seemed to remind me of you, is a doctor now, in Vancouver."

The oldest boy. His son? Maybe, maybe not, and he realized he would never know. It was only Jean who'd said Elaine was pregnant. Could have been wrong. False alarm, maybe. Well, better not to know.

"And your other children?"

"All fine. Married and living all over Canada. One even

in the United States." She laughed. "We've had nothing but good luck since the thirties. Saskatchewan, and most of the people. Seemed as though we had all our bad luck in those ten years, and then the Lord relented. Do you believe that?"

"Could be. I know of no other explanation for the strange and absurd things that happen in this world."

"And you? You've had good fortune, too."

"The best. Before you ask, I never married."

Genuine concern. "What a shame. Oh God, what you've missed! But why?"

Well, here it was. On the line. He couldn't tell her he'd missed his one good chance. That she had spoiled him for other women.

"I'm sorry," she said. "I shouldn't have said that. I'm sure there are lots of advantages to staying single, when you have interesting work, know so many interesting people." With a touch of sadness she added, "Some people are made to be part of a team. Others are better suited to single harness."

And so they sat in silence with their thoughts. He was a boy again, and she a girl. But the years had taken care of that all right.

"I went over to the school." A spoken thought.

For a moment she lost her composure. "Hughie, why did you come back?"

"I had to."

"Did you ever think of me during all those years?"

"Every day."

"But you never wrote or anything."

"I couldn't, that's all, I couldn't. I felt too – damn it, too guilty."

She laughed then. "Oh Hughie, Hughie, but how like you. We were young, thrown together in this place, like two people on an ocean voyage. And then the ship docked. We've both done the things we wanted to do. I'd set my cap for you, you know."

"I don't believe that."

"Anyway, what happens to us is largely our own doing. I was never meant for tragedy."

"No, you weren't. And you never thought of me at all?"

"Too busy – children, politics, a loving husband to take care of me." She stopped. "I'm lying, of course. First love you never forget. Whenever there's hoar-frost clinging to the wires and the stems of grass and the air is clear and cold, I think of our walks together. I was a wild, impulsive girl, ready for love. You didn't seduce me, Hughie, I seduced you. And you know something? I'm glad I did."

"So am I." He stood up and held out his hand to her. She took it. "Goodbye, Elaine."

"Goodbye, Hughie." She was smiling. "And this is really goodbye. May God go with you."

He left her then. Walked straight towards the school along a weedy path, past some houses that he knew, and before he realized it he was walking past the Walpers' house, or rather where it had been. Nothing there now but a slight hole in the ground full of weeds. Gone.

And suddenly he felt better. Elaine was right. His life had been a success and this place had helped make it so. This place and these people, whom he'd detested. All part of him.

As he drove back to Saskatoon the feeling grew. Past the fields of grain and the small towns huddled along the tracks. This place was part of him, and would always be. A rough place, a stern place, where it was a monumental task just to survive. And it had given him some of its strength.

Oh, no, he didn't want to come back here to live. Other places were part of him, too, and other people. And suddenly he was anxious to see his brothers and sisters again. To argue with them, and fight. He couldn't tell them how he felt. They'd never understand, he knew.

When he reached the house on River Crescent and stopped in front of it, he felt there was something wrong. And then his sister Gwen came out of the house and down the walk to the car.

He knew from her face that something was very wrong.

"What's up, Gwen?" he asked.

"It's Father. He's gone, Hugh. A heart attack."

"No! When?"

"Just after you left. It was fast and merciful. His old heart just stopped. We didn't know where to reach you."

"And Mother?"

"She's in bed. All the life seems to have gone from her." She put her arm around her brother's shoulder. "You can cry, Hugh. It's all right to cry."

Chapter Seventeen

It was time to go. Hugh knew that. He had commitments in the east. A documentary for the film board on the life of Tommy Douglas. His New York agent had been talking about an autobiography. And, being a writer, the information he'd got about his parents made that prospect more enticing. Yeah, it was time to get back to work.

But somehow he was reluctant to go. He'd hated the idea of coming back to the prairies and his family, yet now he wasn't anxious to go. Maybe it was the prairie itself. So green and prosperous. Not a duststorm in sight. Prosperous farms, contented people. What a contrast to the devastation, frustration, suspicion, and hatred that had prevailed in the thirties.

And his family. He was standing on the lawn looking over the river-bank and the broad river, and breathing the crisp clean air of the prairies when Gwen approached him.

"It's a lovely sight, isn't it?" she said.

"Yeah, I guess it is. One of the world's big rivers. How's Mother?"

"Pretty good, considering. She's ready. Made me promise that we wouldn't hook her up to any life-support systems."

"Not much point. When one doesn't want to live, one should die. We all will soon enough. 'Never send to know for whom the bell tolls,' eh?"

Gwen laughed. "You've been here only a week and you've picked up the 'eh' habit."

"Why not? It's a handy word. No worse than 'you know' or 'actually.' They're all verbal punctuation marks."

"I suppose you'll be leaving soon."

"Tomorrow. Reservation's made. A couple of phone calls brought me back to reality. I was against this reunion - you know that - but now I'm glad I came."

"Oh? I'm curious to know why."

"Well, there were some things I had to get straight in my mind. About the prairies and its people. I never had a decent chance with - well, this place and my family."

"In what way?"

"I've been thinking about it. Poverty mostly. That worst of all human conditions. Poverty and the frustration and humiliation that go with it. That's part of it. And I never should have been born on the prairies."

"Why?"

"Well, it's a great place for farmers, like Dad, and salesmen, like Tom. My God, the place was made for salesmen. People needed everything. And for businessmen. But not for writers."

"It is now."

"So I hear. But in those days a person might as well have tried to be a deep-sea diver here as a writer. I always felt out of place somehow. Does that make sense?"

"I think so. And the family?"

"Out of place there, too."

"Me, too. I'm not a busy-body, really, but - well, I just thought we should get together. Maybe it was a premonition about Father. I don't know."

"Well, anyway, thanks. We all owe you. Now I'm going to say goodbye to Ma. As Tom would say, 'It ain't gonna be easy.' "

Hugh went into the house and up the wide stairway and into his mother's room. Olive got up from where she'd been sitting beside the bed.

"How is she?" Hugh asked.

"About the same. Right now she's back on the homestead."

"I'll stay with her for a while."

"Good. I could use a cup of coffee."

Hugh sat down on the bedside chair and held his mother's thin white hand. She was in a half-sitting position and turned her head towards him.

"Hughie, Hughie."

What do you say to a dying woman?

"Do you want anything, Ma?"

"No. I don't need a thing." Then silence, and then, "You know, Hughie, all the years have kind of got squashed together in my mind. Just now I was on the homestead giving you and Tom a bath in the round galvanized tub. We had to be careful of the water."

"Yeah. I hated those baths. Especially getting my hair washed. Soap in my eyes."

"And then you'd holler. My, you did have a big voice for a little one. I'm sorry, Hughie."

"Sorry? For what?"

"For what happened to you when Alvin was born. You were such a sensitive little boy, and you needed your mother. But I was too busy."

"Ma! I had the best boyhood. . . ."

"No, you didn't. You were special and I knew it." She sighed heavily. "But I did my best."

"Of course you did." He leaned forward and kissed her, tears in his eyes.

"Where's Tom?" she asked after a while.

"He'll be here soon."

"He'll look after everything when I'm gone." She sighed. "He's always been such a one to look after things. He looked after you, too."

"He did?"

"Don't you remember when that Bruce Gordon chased you home? Tom punched him on the nose." She laughed a thin laugh. "Should have heard Bruce holler then."

"I'd forgotten that."

"Yes, it's easier to remember the times when he was mean to you. Are you going back to Toronto?"

"Yes, that's my home."

"And my home is here. I used to think I wanted to return

to Toronto to retire, but I guess I just became a prairie flower. The prairie was his dream, and how I hated it at first. But it rather gets into your blood."

"Yes, it does."

"Don't hang around here waiting for me to die, Hughie. Get on with your life. I'm dead now. Like poor Sam Aikens."

"Sam Aikens?"

"A neighbour of ours. He had one of those circular saws rigged up on wheels and he cut our poplar poles for firewood. Well, one day that saw flew off and cut him almost in half."

"How terrible!"

"Below the heart and stomach. He lasted about an hour, but he knew he was dead. We did our best for him. He talked to us. Oh, the farm was a cruel place."

She closed her eyes then, and Hugh thought she was asleep. Then, "I've had such a good life. Will was such a good man. My, he was a good man. And my children, just look at them. All but Alvin." And the tears ran down her cheeks. She turned her head away and entered a world where he knew he could not follow.

And so he left her forever.

Tom said, "I suppose you got to get back to your life in Toronto, little brother. I'll take care of things here. Ma's in good hands. We'll have her up and around in no time."

They were walking along a path by the river and had come to a fallen birch. Tom perched on the trunk and lit up a cigar.

"I know you'll take care of things, Tom. You always have." He broke off a dead stick and threw it into the bush. "And I want you to know I'm grateful for what you've done for the folks, and for me."

"You?"

"Come on. You know damned well if you hadn't quit school and gone to work in 1929, I wouldn't have been able to finish high school." This was hard for Hugh to say. "I'm aware of your sacrifice."

"Sacrifice! That was no sacrifice. I hated school. Oh,

I was good enough at it, but it always seemed teachers took so much time explaining the obvious. I could read and do arithmetic and write. What more did I need? They didn't have any courses in salesmanship. And you got your facts wrong. I quit school in 1927."

"What? Then – "

"Depression had nothing to do with it. I wanted to go to work, little brother."

"Well." Hugh let out a long breath. "I'll be damned. And all these years I've been thinking. . . ."

"You mean you been worrying about it? Thinking you done me wrong?"

"Something like that."

"Hell, no. Put your mind at rest, little brother."

"There's another thing. Do you think maybe you could stop calling me little brother?"

"That bother you, too? Well, I'm damned. Sure I'll quit, uh, Hugh. Hell, I don't think I ever called you that before. Either squirt or little brother or worse. Well, no more." He held out his big right hand.

Hugh took it. "Anyway, quitting school obviously didn't hurt your career."

"Not so's you'd notice. Say, after – well, all this – we're taking a trip east. Just the wife and me. Haven't been to Toronto since the last mayors' convention."

"Yeah, I missed you then. I was in New York. This time we'll do the town."

"Deal." Tom stood up and looked over the river towards downtown Saskatoon. "You know, this is a great little city – when you get to know it, that is. My city."

Hugh looked, too. "I agree. Never thought I would. Do you think I should stay for a while? I mean with Ma sick?"

"Not if you've got work to do. Ma might hang on for months. If she gets worse I'll phone you. You can be here in a few hours. I'm hoping you'll come back more often. All those years. . . ."

"Yes, yes, of course I will."

Tom looked at him sideways. "How were things out there in Harman?"

"You remember Harman?"

"Oh yes. I drove you out there, remember?"

"Of course. Well, things are just fine in Harman. In fact, big brother, things are fine all over."

"Why don't you come out to the ranch and see the kids?" Olive asked Gwen. They were still awkward with each other, like a couple of middleweights feeling each other out.

"I'd love to," Gwen replied. "But I have a speaking engagement in Chicago day after tomorrow."

"Chicago. We went there for our honeymoon. What are you going to speak about?"

"Uh, child psychology, actually."

"Child psychology?" Olive was about to say, "What in hell do you know about kids?" But she didn't. "I could have used some of that a few years ago."

"You did all right. A person with good common sense, such as you have, doesn't need much advice. It's the others who tend to make a mess of it."

They were silent, each realizing they were getting close to a bad subject. Then Olive said, "Do you miss not having any kids?"

Her sister lit another cigarette. "Miss it? Of course I do. But I've done what I wanted to do. My life has other compensations."

"It sure has." And then she blurted it out. "Gwen, why did you never get married?"

"Because the man I loved was killed in that rotten war!"

"What? And here I thought. . . ."

"That you had ruined my life by stealing my boyfriend?"

"Well?"

"That was a rotten thing to do, Olive. But I suspect that over the years it's bothered you more than it has me. You may have thought you'd contributed to me being a frustrated old virgin. You didn't. I'm neither frustrated nor a virgin."

"Whew! That'll hold me. Our lives are so different."

"True. But equally interesting in their own way. I wouldn't change mine and I'm sure you wouldn't change yours."

"Well, sometimes I think Clayton is more interested in his damned cows than in me and the kids. That and younger women."

"I'm sorry. How long?"

"How long has that been going on? How long have we been married? But he's been a good provider, a good father, and really a kind man. It's just that he's got this thing. . . ." She laughed. "No pun intended." She drew a deep breath. "I'm glad we had this talk."

"Me, too. And I will come to the ranch as soon as possible."

They both knew she never would and they were both satisfied.

Shawn said, "I'm going to get me a piece of good Saskatchewan land and raise everything we need for survival. When the big bombs start falling, we may have a chance."

"Goodbye, all," Hugh said. He shook hands with his brothers and kissed his sisters. "I'll be back when – when necessary, if I'm still living."

As the airliner lifted off from the runway, he could see the flat land. The roads criss-crossed it in straight lines; he saw the farms with their shelter belts of trees around the buildings. And somewhere down there was Elaine, busy and happy. He hadn't ruined her life. No one but dictators and generals ever ruin anyone's life.

"Well," he said to himself as he settled back in his seat. "That's that."

11/01/03